Eight Life-Enriching Practices of UNITED METHODISTS

Henry H. KNIGHT, III

ABINGDON PRESS/Nashville

EIGHT LIFE-ENRICHING PRACTICES OF UNITED METHODISTS

Copyright © 2001 by Abingdon Press

This book is printed on acid-free paper.

Unless otherwise indicated, Scripture quotations in this publication are from the *Holy Bible: New Revised Standard Version*, copyright © 1989 by the Division of Christian Education of the National Council of the Churches of Christ in the United States of America, and are used by permission. All rights reserved.

Library of Congress Cataloging-in-Publication Data

Knight, Henry H., 1948-
   Eight life-enriching practices of United Methodists / Henry H. Knight.
      p. cm.
   ISBN 0-687-08734-1 (acid-free paper)
      1. Spiritual life--United Methodist Church (U.S.) I. Title.

BX8349.S68 K63 2001
248.4'876--dc21

                                                              2001033653

02 03 04 05 06 07 08 09 10—10 9 8 7 6 5 4 3 2

MANUFACTURED IN THE UNITED STATES OF AMERICA

Contents

Introduction

JOHN WESLEY FREQUENTLY linked our happiness with our being holy. By "holy" he did not mean the kind of holier-than-thou piety that turns off so many people. At its heart, holiness for Wesley was simply love—loving God and our neighbor as God has loved us. We were created for love, but we do not love as we know we should. We have a problem we cannot solve, a disease we cannot cure. But God has made a way for us in Jesus Christ and will transform our lives through the power of the Holy Spirit. Only when we begin to live this new life of love do we find true happiness and genuine enrichment.

This book is about how we can open our lives to this transforming power. It describes eight practices through which we can enter into a life-changing relationship with God. Some of these are themselves collections of practices. Because there is no single "right way" to do them, I will often provide a number of ways we might begin. It is as we engage in these practices that we find our lives being renewed by the Holy Spirit and receive a deeper fulfillment than we may have dreamed possible.

Wesley called such practices "means of grace." It was the genius of early Methodism to nurture Christian growth by placing the means of grace at the very center of their lives together. Wesley still has much to teach us about Christian formation today, and I shall draw upon his wisdom in the pages that follow.

I hope this book will serve as a doorway to the many excellent contemporary resources on Christian spiritual practices. As you will see, I have enormous respect for writers like Richard Foster, Dallas Willard, Steve Harper, Marjorie Thompson, Robert Mulholland, and Philip Yancey. If my citing these and many others in the notes leads you to sample the richness of their writings, I shall rejoice.

Moreover, I hope this book will be a doorway into the Christian life itself. These practices are life enriching because they nourish our lives with God, lives marked by joy, peace, faith, hope, and—above all—love. Wesley was right: Nothing less than this will give us true happiness. The good news is God offers it to us as a gift, if we will only receive it.

I am especially grateful to Sherry Habben and Brian Germano, themselves skilled teachers of Christian formation in the local church, for reading this material and offering sound advice. As always, I am grateful to my wife, Eloise, who not only helped get this manuscript in shape but also has been an encouragement throughout.

Abbreviations

Because John Wesley's writings are frequently referenced in the notes, the following abbreviations are used:

Works   *The Works of John Wesley* (BiCentennial Edition), published initially by Oxford University Press and continued by Abingdon Press. This new and as yet unfinished edition was begun in 1975. Each volume is edited by a leading scholar in Wesleyan Studies.

Works (J)   *The Works of the Rev. John Wesley, M.A.* (Jackson Edition), published in 14 volumes by Thomas Jackson in 1829–31.

Notes   *Explanatory Notes Upon the New Testament*, originally published by John Wesley in 1755.

NEW LIFE

Chapter 1

A Hunger for God

IF YOU COULD travel back to eighteenth-century England to see firsthand the beginnings of Methodism, what would you find? You might come across a preacher, most likely a lay person, proclaiming the good news of Jesus Christ to a crowd in the open air. Or, if you arrived on the right day, you might find a large gathering of Methodists attending a quarterly society meeting and celebrating a love feast. You might even run across an annual conference where John and Charles Wesley discussed with other preachers what they would preach and how they would nurture the growing movement. But you would definitely find small groups of Methodists led by laity who were meeting together weekly to encourage one another in keeping a set of practices that assisted their growth as Christians. For the most part, these Methodists would not be persons of extraordinary gifts or talents, but ordinary people with all the struggles, hopes, sufferings, and joys that come with everyday life. What distinguished them from their contemporaries was their following a discipline of daily devotion, communal gathering, public worship, and outreach to their neighbors.

This was what made one a Methodist: a commitment to keep a set of regular practices (a "discipline") and to attend a weekly meeting to share how keeping these practices was going. These early Methodists were convinced that through following this discipline they would grow in the knowledge and love of God and love for their neighbor as well. They had a deep hunger for God and saw these practices as a means to satisfy that hunger.

Early Methodists illustrated well this point made by Richard Foster concerning spiritual disciplines: "We need not be well advanced in matters of theology to practice the Disciplines. Recent converts—for that matter people who have not yet turned their lives over to Jesus Christ—should practice them. The primary requirement is a longing after God."[1] Do you have a longing for God? Do you want to know and love God more fully, as you are known and loved by God? Then these life-enriching practices can be a means for you to develop a deeper relationship with God, just as they were for the first Methodists and for countless other Christians over the centuries.

Knowing God

What does it mean to have a relationship with God? We can begin to answer this question by thinking about our relationships with one another. While there is much that could be said, there are at least two elements of any relationship that are essential.

First, you must in some way meet the other person and maintain contact over time. For short, I have called this *presence*[2] although a human relationship does not always require physical presence—people maintain relationships through writing letters, telephoning, and now e-mail. But a relationship does require some means of conversation or at least contact. There is, of course, an advantage to actually being together: Actions can be joined to words. Persons can then share common experiences such as a meal or a movie, a baseball game or a shopping trip.

Second, a relationship means you come to know another person as a distinct personality, what I have called his or her *identity*. While each of us may have more or less in common with others, no two of us are entirely the same. We are all unique. As we get to know someone, we become increasingly aware of what makes up that person. We learn about personality traits, background, and various likes and dislikes. Above all, we begin to know the person's character. One reason we are so often disappointed in the failings of public figures is because we thought we knew them, but what we really knew was their image. In a true relationship, we come increasingly to know another as he or she really is.

When we move from human relationships to God, we encounter an immediate problem: How do we experience God's presence and identity? As humans, we can see, hear, or touch one another. But God is spirit—how, then, do we know one whom we cannot literally see, hear, or touch?

John Wesley said we know God by *faith*, which is "the assurance of things hoped for, the conviction of things not seen" (Heb. 11:1). He understood faith to be a "spiritual" sense, a gift of the Holy Spirit analogous to our five senses. Just as our senses of touch, taste, speaking, hearing, and smell put us in contact with physical reality, faith is a capacity by which we "discerneth God and the things of God."[3] It is faith that enables us to encounter God as a real and active presence in our lives and world. Faith, then, is more than believing that there is a God—it is knowing God, in some ways as you would know another person.

But who is this God? What of God's identity? We cannot know who God is simply through our own experience, for that is notoriously deceptive. By ourselves we then create a god to meet our perceived wants or needs, which may not at all be the way God actually is. However, we can know who God is through what God has done, first in creation and the story of Israel, and finally in Jesus Christ.

Christians believe God actually entered human history through Jesus of Nazareth. When we are asked, "What is God like?" we point to Jesus. His teaching, healing, casting out demons, and reaching out to those in need or on the margins of society are seen not only as human actions but also as divine. His death on the cross is the ultimate expression of God's infinite love for us. Charles Wesley puts it this way:

> O Love divine, what hast thou done!
> The immortal God hath died for me!
> The Father's coeternal Son bore all my
> sins upon the tree.
> Th' immortal God for me hath died:
> My Lord, my Love, is crucified![4]

Because he is risen from the dead, Jesus is alive, not only revealing God's identity but also, through the Holy Spirit, manifesting God's presence. As Luke Timothy Johnson says, for Jesus to live means he "is not simply a figure of the past . . . but a person in the present; not merely a memory that we can analyze and manipulate, but an agent who can confront and instruct us." We can not only "learn *about* him" but can "continue to learn *from* him."[5] No wonder then that Christians have understood a "relationship with Jesus" to be a "relationship with God" or have seen their relationship with the triune God to be "through Christ" and "in the Spirit."

Relationships are not one-time encounters but are lived out over time. The primary way we remain in relationship with God is through participation in practices of worship, devotion, community, and outreach. As we do these things, we come to know and love God more deeply, and as a result we grow in our faith. The most profound and life-changing aspect of this relationship is our experiencing again and again God's love for us in Jesus Christ.

What Salvation Really Is

Some readers may be wondering why I have emphasized having a relationship with God. It is one thing, they might say, to trust in Christ for our salvation, but another to enter into an ongoing relationship with God that requires our active participation. Isn't salvation simply being forgiven for our sins, so that when we die we do not receive the punishment we deserve but instead live forever? The short answer is no, that is not what salvation is, at least at its heart.

Christians have long affirmed that humans are created in the image of God, though they have had varying ideas about what that exactly means. They have also agreed that because humanity has fallen into sin, the image of God in each of us has been seriously damaged. While they use different language and disagree over the extent of the damage, they all would agree with Cornelius Plantinga that because of sin life is "not the way it's supposed to be."[6]

Because "God is love" (1 John 4:8), Wesley believed that to be in the image of God would be to love as God loves— to love God and our neighbor as well as all of creation. Our problem is that we find this hard to do, and it is hard to do because of who we are. Wesley said the image of God in us is totally corrupted, afflicted by sin much as someone is ravaged by a disease that is both incurable and terminal. As a result, our thoughts and actions, understanding and dispositions are so caught in sin that we cannot extricate ourselves. It distorts our relationships, skews all our decisions, and harms friend and stranger alike. It even harms our own selves.

13

Is Wesley's diagnosis of this disease too severe? He is not saying that everything we do is "wrong," but that sin—a lack of love for God, neighbor, and creation, and a putting of self into the center of our lives instead of God—is at the root of and is inextricably woven in all we say and do. I invite you to consider the effects.

As you survey the "big picture" of life on our planet, are things the way they are supposed to be? Isn't it the case that in politics or business, entertainment or the environment, nations far away or communities close to home, something seems to have gone radically and tragically wrong? We could—though this is more troubling—look into our own hearts and lives, examining how we treat one another or what values direct our lives and influence our decisions. At the very least, perhaps we can agree that things are badly awry, and a vital part of what is missing is a consistent, caring love.

The early Methodists certainly thought so. Those new to the movement had become "awakened" to their condition. They saw themselves as sinners, separated from God, and longed to experience forgiveness and reconciliation. They had what Wesley called the "faith of a servant," seeking to obey God as best they could and in the process discovering just how strong sin was in their lives.

This is a disconcerting discovery for most of us. We like to think that we are in control of our own lives and that everything is well in hand. What being "awakened" does is show us that while we can struggle against sin, we cannot overcome it. We do not have the freedom we think we do. We need help that only God can provide.

Polls show that large numbers of Americans believe Christianity teaches that you must be good to go to heaven. There are many in the church who understand the Christian life as dutiful obedience or just trying to do the best you can. The early Methodists were under no such illusions. The "faith of a servant" was part of the process of salvation but was not the goal. It was not the end of the journey but an important first step on the way.

It might seem that the goal would be knowing that God through Jesus Christ forgave their sins. Certainly the experience of forgiveness (or *justification*) was a powerful, life-changing event. They were given this forgiveness as a free gift of God that they neither deserved nor earned. It was, they would say, by grace alone, understood as God's unmerited favor. As a result, they were reconciled to this God who loved them so much even to die for them. They found a new faith (the faith of a child of God) that enabled them to trust in Christ. They received a new sense of their own worth and dignity, which could only come from knowing God's great love for them in Christ. And their motive for serving God began to change as well, from dutiful obedience to loving gratitude for all that God had done for them in Christ.

It would be understandable for something this profound to be seen as Christian salvation. Many have done so. Yet for early Methodists justification was a crucial element of salvation but could not be its goal. Forgiveness frees us from the guilt of sin but does not free us from its power. As long as the power of sin remains unbroken, then our lives are only marginally changed—we still find ourselves caught in the same unhealthy habits, the same destructive relationships, and living out of the same distorted values.

Dallas Willard has called this understanding of a Christian as forgiven but unchanged a "bar code faith." The scanners at the cash registers read only the bar codes on products. If you put the bar code for dog food on ice cream, the scanner will read "dog food" without regard to the actual content of the package.

A "bar code faith" works much the same way. Through some action on our part—having faith, joining a church, performing a ritual—we do what is necessary to receive forgiveness. This gives us a new "bar code." God ignores the contents of the package and responds to the new "bar code" with forgiveness. Some of Christ's righteousness is shifted "to our account . . . and all our debts are paid." For some traditions, repeated acts are necessary to keep our "debts paid up"; for others all is paid for at once with "the initial scan. But the essential thing in either case is the forgiveness of sins," with the "payoff for having faith and being 'scanned'" coming "at death and after." Our present life "has no necessary connection with being a Christian as long as the 'bar code' does its job."[7]

Living over two hundred years before bar codes and scanners, the early Methodists were well aware of this understanding of salvation. They rejected it for selling salvation short. God has a much bigger and more wonderful plan for us than this. God is not content to leave us at the mercy of this disease of sin but instead seeks to do in our lives what we cannot do for ourselves. God wants to restore in each of us the image of God so that love will govern our hearts and lives and begin to heal our relationships with God, neighbor, and creation. Salvation not only includes justification (our forgiveness and acceptance by God) but *sanctification*, our inward renewal by the Holy Spirit. According to Wesley, this was the "end of Christ's coming," a "restoration not only to the favour, but likewise to the image of God; implying not barely deliverance from sin but the being filled with the fullness of God." For Wesley, "nothing short of this is Christian religion."[8]

The Gift of New Life

When Jesus was asked which commandment in the law given by God to Israel was the greatest, he answered, "'You shall love the Lord your God with all your heart, and with all your soul, and with all your mind.' This is the greatest and first commandment. And a second is like it: 'You shall love your neighbor as yourself'" (Matt. 22:37-39).

John Wesley was convinced that whatever God commands, through grace God would enable us to do. Thus, this command to whole-hearted love "is not only a direction what I shall do, but a promise of what God will do in me."[9] For Wesley, God's grace is more than unmerited favor; it is life-transforming power, not only what "God does *for us* in forgiving our sins," but also "the great work which God does *in us*, in renewing our fallen nature."[10]

This transformation of our lives does not occur all at once; it is a process of growth. It begins with *regeneration* (or the *new birth*) in which the Holy Spirit breaks the hold of sin on our lives and sets us free to begin loving God and our neighbor. Regeneration occurs simultaneously with justification and begins the process of sanctification, in which we grow in the knowledge and love of God.

The culmination of sanctification is what Wesley called *Christian perfection* or *entire sanctification*.[11] The term *perfection* is troubling to most of us because our normal definition implies a kind of absolute state that can be neither improved nor changed. The reason is that our English word *perfection* is drawn from a Latin predecessor. Wesley is using instead the Greek understanding found in the New Testament and rooted in centuries of early Christian tradition. He variously describes Christian perfection as "the humble, gentle, patient love of God and our neighbour, ruling our tempers, words, and actions,"[12] having "all the mind which was in Christ, enabling us to walk as Christ walked," and the "renewal of the heart in the whole image of God."[13] It is, in short, not an absolute perfection but a perfection in love.

This perfection is meant for everyone. You do not have to do extraordinary things or possess special qualities to qualify, though you do need to be in a relationship with God, growing in sanctification. Robin Maas aptly describes Christian perfection as *"loving to full capacity*—however small or great that capacity may be." It is being "filled to the brim with a yearning for God."[14]

Contrary to our usual way of thinking, this means that we can grow in perfection. We can enlarge our capacity to love by coming to recognize more fully occasions to love and by learning from experience as we put this love into practice. Filled with God's love, we can continue to grow in our ability to see the world and our neighbor as God does. Wesley's advice is appropriate: "When ye have attained a measure of perfect love, when God has . . . enabled you to love him with all your heart and with all your soul, think not of resting there. . . . Therefore the voice of God . . . to the children of God is, 'Go forward.'"[15]

Go forward! This is what Wesley urges us to do wherever we find ourselves on our Christian journey. Continue to grow in love, he exhorts, and strengthen your relationship with God. This book is designed to help us do that. It will describe the practices that enrich our lives because they satisfy our hunger for God and open us to receive all the life that God seeks to give us. As we engage in these practices, the Holy Spirit will not only draw us closer to God but also remake us so that we increasingly mirror in our own lives the great and wonderful love of God, which comes to us in Jesus Christ.

Discussion Questions

1. Richard Foster spoke of a "longing for God." What kinds of "longings" do people have in our culture today? What difference would it make in our lives for us to have a longing for God?

2. How does "knowing" God differ from "knowing about" God? What are some ways we can know God?

3. Who is God? What does the story of what God has done in creation and for our salvation tell us about God's character?

4. The New Testament proclaims that Jesus was crucified and is risen from the dead. What difference does this make for our lives and world?

5. If a friend asked you what is meant by "salvation," how would you respond?

6. One of the questions asked of every Methodist preacher who has sought full conference membership from Wesley's day to our own is, "Are you going on to perfection?" One bishop, after asking this question, would add, "If not, what are you going on to?" How would you describe the directions our lives frequently take, and in what direction do you believe God would have us go?

Chapter 2

Growing in Grace

M ARTIN THORNTON, a contemporary priest in the Church of England, expressed a certain frustration with the writings of the major Protestant theologians of the first half of the twentieth century. Their books said insightful and admirable things about salvation by grace alone, our acceptance by God just as we are, and the resulting need for us to dwell in Christ, participate in the Christian community, and be faithful disciples. Yet again and again, as he encountered these comments about faithfulness, obedience, participation, and the like, Thornton wrote in the margins the initials "Y.B.H.?" standing for "Yes, but *how?*" If, as they all said, we must respond to this gracious, salvific love of God, then exactly "*how* do ordinary men and women, bankers, typists, farmers and nurses" become and live as disciples of Jesus Christ?[1]

It was the genius of Wesley's movement to provide a comprehensive answer to the "Yes, but *how?*" question. Early Methodists participated in a rich array of spiritual practices that enabled them to grow in their relationship with God. Their engagement in these practices was not an alternative to grace but rather because of it—not a way of making grace unnecessary but of receiving it and responding to it.

As he developed this approach to Christian growth, Wesley found himself in the middle of two opposing understandings of salvation, neither of which was satisfactory. On one side were those who insisted salvation was by grace alone, not by works; therefore, we need do nothing but have faith to be saved. Those on the extreme of this position even saw good works as irrelevant to being a Christian. If Christ has done everything necessary for our salvation, why should we even be concerned with our faithfulness or morality?

On the other side were those who emphasized morality. To be a Christian was to live a good life and do good works. Grace was important for our forgiveness, but they feared an overemphasis on grace would undercut biblical admonitions to moral obedience.

Wesley believed neither of these views because both misunderstood the grace of God. He saw grace as *relational*, in that it both *enables* us to enter a relationship with God and then *invites* us to do so. It enables us because without grace we could not be able on our own; the power of sin in our lives is too strong. It invites us because, thus enabled, we must respond to God's reaching out in love to us through Christ and the Spirit. Relationships by their very nature involve two-way participation.

Drawing on the experience of new birth, Wesley describes the enabling power of grace by reminding Christians how God worked in their lives. God "did not take away your understanding; but enlightened and strengthened it." Nor did God "destroy any of your affections; rather they were more vigorous than before." God, says Wesley, "did not *force* you; but being *assisted* by his grace you, like Mary, *chose* the better part."[2] Grace, in short, does not overcome us but enlivens us and enables us to enter into a relationship with God.

Grace invites us because God seeks our free response to God's love. To overpower us would prevent us from loving freely, as God does; it would undermine the whole point of salvation, which is for us to be in God's image once again. God seeks partners, not puppets, whose worship and service are not compelled but joyfully given. This, says Philip Yancey, "is the miracle of God's condescension, his humble willingness to share power and offer us full partnership in the mission of transforming the world."[3]

How We Become Drawn Away from God

To say God invites us into a relationship implies that we can decline God's invitation. We often envision the Christian life as a clear choice: God makes it possible, offers it to us, and then we freely make our decision. Yet Christian spiritual writers through the centuries have warned that things are not this simple—we can be drawn away from a relationship with God almost unawares. There are subtle but definite dangers to the Christian life.

Wesley emphasized a number of these dangers. Two examples are antinomianism ("against the law"), which argues that salvation by grace frees us from moral or ethical commands, and legalism, which sees salvation as largely through obeying the moral law. These had to do with how we understand grace and salvation.

Two other dangers are even more harmful because they lead us to think we are in a relationship with God when we are not. The first of these is *formalism*.[4] Formalists believe they will go to heaven if they fulfill their religious obligations, such as attending church or making a financial contribution to the church. Instead of a means to loving and serving God, these become ends in themselves. Wesley says that when you ask dishonest tradesmen if they are Christians or if they are going to heaven, nine out of ten will reply, "As good a Christian as yourself! Go to heaven? Yes, sure! *For I keep my church* as well as any man."[5] Formalism replaces a transforming relationship with God with "keeping church."

While they may assent to church teachings, formalists lack the faith to seek God or trust in Christ; they may know *about* God, but they do not know God. It is possible they never had that faith, but it is also possible they once had it but lost it. The chief reason we never acquire faith or lose the faith we have is due to what Wesley called dissipation.

In its common usage, dissipation referred to an irresponsible lifestyle: The young aristocrat who spent his time partying, drinking, and the like was said to be living a dissipated life. Wesley expands the definition to encompass anyone who "is habitually inattentive to the presence and will of his Creator."[6] Dissipation is "the art of forgetting God."[7]

Note that Wesley does not see the problem as God's absence but rather our inattention to God's presence. This inattention is due to our being "encompassed on all sides with persons and things that tend to draw us from our centre."[8] It is not simply temptation to sin that dissipates us; just as often, it is those things we would call good. We are faced with deadlines and have many responsibilities; we juggle work and family; our minds are filled with a thousand things to remember to do as well as multiple worries and concerns. Pastors, who have so many demands on their time, are not immune, and constant church activity itself can draw us from God. Philip Yancey speaks of how "an accumulation of distractions—a malfunctioning computer, bills to pay, an upcoming trip, a friend's wedding, the general busyness of life—gradually edges God away from the center of my life."[9]

The result of prolonged dissipation is a "practical atheism"—we still believe there is a God but live our lives as if we did not. Our belief in God simply makes no difference, and so our religion becomes a kind of going through the motions.

The cure for dissipation and formalism is a faith that enables us to know and love God. As we have seen, this faith is itself a gracious work of the Holy Spirit; we have it not by trying harder but by receiving it as a gift. How, then, do we remain open to receiving faith? And, having received, how do we continue to retain and nurture this faith, given that we are continually threatened by dissipation?

This was precisely the reason early Methodists, as well as Christians before and since, have kept to a discipline. The purpose of spiritual discipline is to keep us focused on God and our neighbor when so much in life threatens to draw us away. Practicing a devotional life, corporate worship, community participation, and outreach to others are ways to maintain and grow in our relationship with God.

I shall say more about this discipline in a later chapter. Here we should note that it was not only having this discipline but also being held accountable to it that enabled the early Methodists to keep focused on God and neighbor. Attending a weekly meeting in which individuals give an account of how they have kept to the discipline is a strong incentive to do so, as well as an opportunity to help each other through sharing advice and experiences.

How We Confuse God with Our Feelings

I mentioned there were two especially harmful dangers to the Christian life. The second is *enthusiasm*, a word that meant something different in Wesley's day than it does in ours. When students or laity assure me that their churches are in no danger of enthusiasm, it is clear the definition has changed!

To Wesley, enthusiasm was a kind of imaginary religion in which persons "imagine themselves to be so influenced by the Spirit of God as in fact they are not."[10] Enthusiasts would include those who constantly seek after new experiences or new gifts, who believe God dictates the words they speak (and are therefore never wrong), or who see every impulse or feeling they have as a direction from God.

The enthusiast, in short, confuses having a relationship with God with having certain feelings or gifts. Wesley certainly does not deny that our relationship with God can produce distinct feelings. What he does deny is that the absence of these feelings means there is no relationship with God. Nor does their absence mean we haven't received the new birth: We do not have to *feel* loving in order to *be* a loving person.

Instead, he raises a crucial question: How do you know a particular feeling or impulse is from God? Enthusiasts simply assume that because they have a feeling or impulse, it must come from God. But Wesley could think of a couple of other plausible sources: It could come from Satan or be generated by our own sinful self. Wesley certainly believes God does generate new experiences, give us gifts, and lead us in particular directions. The issue is how to test the spirits.

To this he offers three pieces of helpful advice. First, we should consult Scripture, which provides "a general rule, applicable to all particular cases: 'The will of God is our sanctification' . . . that we should be inwardly and outwardly holy."[11] The Holy Spirit, often in subtle ways, will assist our reason as we examine what is God's will in a particular instance in light of this rule.

Second, he suggests we not use the expression "I want to know what is the will of God." It is too open-ended and encourages some to believe that almost anything could be God's will. It is not the tragic instances of people thinking God is telling them to commit murder or suicide that Wesley has in mind. Rather, it is more like the wealthy investor seeking God's will in order to attain the best return or the consumer seeking God's guidance on what to purchase next. Wesley proposes we ask the question in a more scriptural manner: "I want to know what will be most for my improvement, and what will make me most useful."[12] That is, what aids in my growth in love and other fruit of the Spirit, and what enables me to serve God more fully?

Third, he warns us to beware "of imagining you shall obtain the end without using the means conducive to it." While God can act apart from the means of grace, we "have no reason to think" God will.[13] Therefore, we should use all the means of grace God has given us to enable our growth as Christians.

The reason means of grace such as searching the Scripture and participating in the Lord's Supper help us avoid enthusiasm is that they tell us who God is; that is, they enable us to know God's identity. Through practicing these means of grace we encounter again and again the story of what God has done in creation and redemption. We are continually reminded of the promises of God, which give us hope, and the character of God that is love. To know who God is gives us a way to determine which experiences or "leadings" are from God and which are not.

What Are the Means of Grace?

Wesley defines means of grace as "outward signs, words, or actions ordained of God, and appointed for this end—to be the *ordinary* channels" of conveying "preventing, justifying, or sanctifying grace."[14] Means of grace, then, are practices we do—"outward, words, or actions"—that the Holy Spirit then uses to convey grace. They enable and invite our participation in a relationship with God that will transform our lives and lead to growth as Christians.

Because God establishes means of grace for this purpose, they are the normal and regular ("ordinary") ways we grow in our relationship with God and neighbor. This by no means rules out God's doing an extraordinary work in our lives. Wesley in fact believes the Spirit works in unusual ways—on occasion he or those he preached to would fall to the ground under the Spirit's power. But even recognizing that as a work of the Holy Spirit (and not some other spirit) requires a regular, disciplined practice of the means of grace.

Since means of grace convey preventing (or prevenient) and justifying grace as well as sanctifying grace, one does not have to wait until one is a Christian to use them. Anyone with even the slightest degree of faith can begin to practice them, regardless of his or her current relationship with God. Likewise, we never reach a point where we no longer need means of grace—to say that would be equivalent to saying we no longer need a relationship with God. They mean more to us, not less, as we grow in our Christian lives.

Wesley divides the means of grace into two categories.[15] The *instituted* means are ordained by God to be used by all Christians in every period in history and all human cultures. These were all practiced by Jesus, who commanded his disciples to use them as well. There are five instituted means of grace:

1. Prayer: personal, family, public; extemporaneous and written.
2. Searching the Scriptures by reading, meditating, hearing; hearing the preached word.
3. The Lord's Supper.
4. Fasting, or abstinence.
5. Christian conference, which includes conversations that are edifying or otherwise minister grace to hearers.

Wesley does not consistently list all five. Clearly the first three—prayer, searching the Scriptures, and the Lord's Supper—are preeminent and the ones chosen for discussion in his sermon "The Means of Grace." But it is significant that the discipline of the early Methodists committed them to practice fasting as well.

Conspicuous in its absence is baptism. Wesley believed baptism and the Lord's Supper to be sacraments, and therefore both were for him unquestionably means of grace. But because baptism is celebrated only once while the Lord's Supper is repeatedly offered, Wesley focused on the latter as the ongoing sacrament in the Christian life. Because today we may renew our Baptismal Covenant (a practice similar in intent to Wesley's Covenant Service), baptism—"and the reaffirmation of our baptismal vows"—will be included in this book as a life-enriching practice.

Wesley's second category was the *prudential* means of grace. This included the small groups and spiritual disciplines, covenant services and love feasts, and above all visiting the sick and all other ways of putting love for our neighbor into practice. Prudential means are simply those practices that God seems to be using in a particular time or place. We should be alert to the ways the Holy Spirit is working in our day and culture. This does not mean that practicing spiritual disciplines and loving our neighbor are themselves optional, but that the specific practices through which we do them may vary. Times change and cultures are diverse, so the Spirit continually reveals new needs to be addressed and leads us in creative ways to meet those needs.

Another set of categories used by Wesley focuses on the object of the means of grace. *Works of piety* are those practices directed to God and would include both public worship and personal devotions. *Works of mercy* are those means of grace directed to the neighbor. These two categories show how the means of grace enable us to put into practice the two great commandments to love God and our neighbor.

The means of grace as practiced by the early Methodists formed a pattern of renewal by enabling them to experience both God's presence and identity. Accountability to a discipline at a weekly meeting counteracted dissipation, opening them to experience the presence of God. Other means of grace, such as searching the Scriptures and the Lord's Supper, disclosed the identity of God. Some, like prayer and covenant services, helped in both ways. Through practicing these means of grace, the early Methodists were able to grow in the knowledge and love of God as well as love for their neighbor.

As we practice these means of grace, the Holy Spirit renews our lives. They are life-enriching practices because through them we become the people we were created to be, increasingly mirroring in our lives the love that is at the heart of God.

Discussion Questions

1. What does the word *grace* mean? How does grace work in our lives?

2. What are some ways we are drawn away from God? How can we avoid it?

3. How can we tell that an experience or sense of direction is from God?

4. What are some examples of "works of piety"? How do they help us grow as Christians?

5. What are some examples of "works of mercy"? How do they help us grow as Christians?

Chapter 3

The First Practice: Prayer

GOD LONGS FOR relationship with us. As Richard
Foster says, God "aches over our distance and preoccupa-
tion" and "mourns that we do not draw near to him."
Weeping "over our obsession with muchness and many-
ness," God "longs for our presence." Inviting us "to come
home to that for which we were created," God's "arms are
stretched wide to receive us," and God's "heart is enlarged to
take us in."[1]

"The key to this home, this heart of God," says Foster, "is
prayer."[2]

John Wesley would agree. He called prayer "the grand
means of drawing near to God." Prayer is so indispensable
to the Christian life that the other means of grace are themselves helpful only "as they are mixed with or prepare us for
this."[3] Prayer, he says, is "the breath of our spiritual life."[4]

A longing of God for fellowship with us and our corre-
sponding need to draw near to God may not be what comes
to your mind when you hear the word *prayer*. This is completely understandable. If we look up *prayer* or *pray* in a
standard English dictionary, we find definitions that revolve
around making requests—entreaties, addressing God with a
petition, and the like. That is, prayer is seen as something
we do to bring about a desired result, sometimes through

seeking divine intervention. This equates prayer with petition.

Petition is one form of prayer but it is not its heart. Prayer is being intentionally in God's presence. The focus of prayer is not on our requests but on the God we love.

According to Robert Mulholland, American culture encourages us to think of prayer in functional terms. We are inclined to understand "prayer as something we *do* in order to produce the results we believe are needed or, rather, to get God to produce the results." We want to know "what works" and how to make our prayers more effective.[5] Most of the Christian books on prayer today seek to answer these questions.

The problem with this functional approach is that we use prayer to keep ourselves in control. We have our own agendas and desires—even our own desperate needs—and we seek to enlist God's help. We remain at the center of our lives, and God is kept on the periphery, close enough to assist but not so close as to fundamentally change our hearts.

What we miss, says Mulholland, is "entering into a deep, vital, transforming relationship with God."[6] Prayer is "primarily relational, not functional."[7] It is designed to bring us close to God so that through that relationship, we might increasingly reflect God's love in our own lives.

This is why Wesley saw prayer as a way of life. Wesley knew (in the words of Steve Harper) that "God does not call us to have a devotional time; God calls us to live a devotional life."[8] While Wesley set aside time for prayer each day, he, like St. Paul, urges us to pray without ceasing so that the "heart is ever lifted up to God, at all times, and in all places."[9] Prayer is how we go through each day in constant awareness of God's presence and in continued gratitude for God's gracious love.

I will say more about how we can learn to pray, both at specified times and "without ceasing." But first we need to examine the difference prayer makes in our lives and world.

The Breath of New Life

As we have seen, Wesley says prayer is "the breath of our spiritual life." With the new birth, the "Spirit or breath of God" is "breathed into the new-born soul; and the same breath which comes from, returns to God."

> As it is continually received by faith, so it is continually rendered back by love, by prayer, and praise, and thanksgiving—love and praise and prayer being the breath of every soul which is truly born of God. And by this new kind of spiritual respiration, spiritual life is not only sustained but increased day by day.[10]

Just as we must inhale air and then exhale in order to live and grow, so must we also receive the life-giving Spirit and then breathe back to God our prayers.

Without prayer, our life with God cannot continue. "Nothing can be more plain," Wesley warns, "than that the life of God in the soul does not continue, much less increase, unless we use all opportunities of communing with God." It is no wonder Wesley believed the "neglect of private prayer" to be the most important cause of Christians losing their faith.[11]

Notice how closely Wesley links thanksgiving, praise, and prayer. "Thanksgiving," he says, "is inseparable from true prayer; it is almost essentially connected with it."[12] This connection is no accident. Thanksgiving is not simply one form of prayer; it is in many ways the foundation of all prayer. We are most likely to ask God for the right things when we stand before God with grateful hearts. Let me explain why.

To give God thanks and praise is at one and the same time to acknowledge who God is and who we are. It is to remember all that God has done in creating our world and saving us through Jesus Christ. It is to thank God for all of life's blessings but most especially for the gift of new life. In the process, we acknowledge as well our need to be saved and to be remade in God's love. Offering praise and thanksgiving to God is the ultimate form of realism.

We cannot enter into this kind of prayer and remain the same. As Richard Foster says, "To pray is to change."[13] Once we acknowledge who God is and recognize our own condition before God, we are faced with things about our lives and world we want to change, and we are strengthened in hope by the promise of God to bring about those changes.

Thus we can truly confess our sin before God. On the basis of God's love for us in Christ for which we give thanks, we can ask God to forgive us and enable us to grow in our Christian lives. Likewise, by identifying that in which we need most to grow, our requests to God (or petitions) will be better informed.

Wesley believed prayer to be absolutely necessary "if we would receive any gift from God."[14] He cites Jesus' promise, "Ask, and it will be given you; search, and you will find; knock, and the door will be opened for you" (Matt. 7:7). We do not receive, he says, because we do not ask. But he also notes that the promise in Matthew is to give us "good things" (Matt. 7:11) and in Luke to "give the Holy Spirit to those who ask" (Luke 11:13). At the heart of our petitions is not our agendas apart from God but the "good things" that God has promised us through Jesus Christ.

Wesley has in mind our seeking such "good things" as forgiveness, new life, assurance, perfect love, and growth in the fruit of the Spirit as well as God's wisdom and guidance.

But he also believes the act of praying for these gifts is itself used by the Holy Spirit to transform our lives. The central purpose of our petitions, he says, is not to convince God to meet our requests but to create "a fit disposition on our part to receive his grace and blessing" and "to increase our desire of the things we ask for."[15]

Yet prayer does more than even this. To be in continual relationship with God through prayers of thanksgiving, praise, confession, and petition is to open ourselves to becoming more like God. As Steve Harper says, "Genuine communion with God enables us to know and share God's heart," flowing outward as compassion for others.[16] According to Richard Foster, prayer also gives us new vision. It teaches us to see things from God's "point of view"—to think what God thinks, desire what God desires, and love what God loves.[17]

Our prayers to God do not remove us from the world so much as they prepare us to engage the world. They increasingly enable us to look upon our neighbor and our world with something like the eyes of God and to shape our lives and actions with the love of God.

Bringing the World to God

It is with these new eyes and this deepened love that we bring the world to God in intercessory prayer.

Intercessory prayer is an act of rebellion. It is a holy dissatisfaction with the status quo, a yearning for God's will to be done on earth as it is in heaven. It is an often-passionate cry to God to change things that are not in accord with God's kingdom.

It is also an act of ministry. Sometimes I hear people say, "Prayer is fine, but I think you need to actually *do* something as well." This is a common attitude toward prayer, but it woefully misunderstands it. Intercessory prayer *is* doing something, and it has definite effects.

First, like other forms of prayer, intercession is a means through which the Holy Spirit shapes the lives of those who pray. Some of the most compassionate people I know are laity who have devoted their lives to intercessory prayer. Their practice of intercession has enabled God to give them a deep sensitivity to human need and tremendous empathy with those for whom they pray. Most of us are not called to a special ministry of intercession, but all of us can practice intercessory prayer. As we do, we will find we are being increasingly conformed to the love that is in Christ.

Second, intercession is often an encouragement to those who know others are praying for them. Even if God does not respond in the way desired, the care expressed by offering prayers for another is frequently beneficial in its effect. Intercession is a concrete witness to the reality of a love that persists through each and every circumstance in life.

Third, intercession has an effect on God. What I mean is this: Because of our prayers, God may choose to act in ways that God otherwise would not. While this may seem to be a controversial statement, the biblical evidence overwhelmingly supports it. For example, Paul asks the Thessalonian church to "pray for us, so that the word of the Lord may spread rapidly and be glorified everywhere, just as it is among you, and that we may be rescued from wicked and evil people" (2 Thess. 3:1-2). Here Paul clearly assumes their prayers will make a difference. Likewise, James teaches "the prayer of the righteous is powerful and effective" (James 5:16).

But perhaps most significant is Jesus' response to his disciples' request to teach them to pray. The Lord's Prayer asks God to bring the kingdom, to provide bread, and to spare us from the time of trial (see Matt. 6:9-13), all clearly presupposing that God answers prayer.

We may wonder why God has chosen to permit our prayers a role in affecting divine activity. The word *role* should be underscored—God is still sovereign, still initiates actions without our participation, and can still answer prayers with a "no" or "not yet" as well as a "yes." Yet it does seem that God wants humanity to be partners to God's mission in the world. Created as we are in God's image, humanity at its best seeks the same things God seeks for the world. As I will show in later chapters, this certainly means active involvement in ministries of social concern, environmental stewardship, and evangelism. But it also means praying for these concerns. Sometimes it seems that God will only act when people show by their fervent prayers that they want God to act.

In fact, it is striking how frequently God answers our prayers with a "yes." A cancer is miraculously healed. A seemingly intractable problem is solved. Confusion over which direction to take has been clarified. Persons separated by anger or bitterness have become reconciled.

What needs should we bring before God? Often our vision needs to be enlarged. Sometimes we may have too limited a concept of what God can do. We may be quite willing to ask God to guide the hand of the surgeon but unwilling to ask God to heal the disease. Our cultural bias against anything that seems unusual or miraculous may inhibit our prayers.

Sometimes we may ourselves have a too limited sphere of concern. We may pray for a friend needing surgery or a family member needing a job, but not for the peace process in Northern Ireland or famine and religious persecution in Somalia. We may lift up in prayer flood victims in our town, but not tornado victims in another state. God's concern spans the globe, and if our lives are to mirror God's, then our prayers should reflect those same concerns. There are, some might say, more needs than we can pray about. But we can choose to intercede for at least some needs far away as well as those close at hand.

Learning to Pray

Most of us are convinced we should pray regularly yet do not find it easy. When asked why, many of us say we are just too busy. It's not only that we cannot find time in our busy schedules to pray as we would like. It's more the constant demands of work and family—the imminent deadlines and never being caught up, the being pulled this way and that by our many responsibilities—that make prayer so difficult.

Even when we find a space for prayer, it becomes hurried, just one more thing to do quickly and check off our list. Often we are tired as well, and so it's hard to find the energy for prayer. This is no way to spend time with a friend, human or divine.

These obstacles to prayer are so prevalent that Bill Hybels calls prayer "an unnatural activity." Underlying our busyness, he says, is our culture of self-reliance, the sense that we have to make it on our own. Because prayer is an admission that we are not self-sufficient, it "flies in the face of those deep-seated values."[18]

Hybels advises us to slow down and spend time with God. What has worked for him, as it has for many others, is to keep a *spiritual journal*. When we slow down enough to write, we slow down enough to pray.[19] Another way to slow down that has worked for me is to intentionally *relax the body and mind*. We do this by closing our eyes, breathing more slowly and deeply, and becoming aware of and releasing muscle tension. Then we turn our thoughts to God.

One advantage to practices that slow us down to pray is they help us *listen* to God. When we think of prayer, we often think of speaking to God. But as Steve Harper reminds us, "the witness of believers for twenty centuries is that

38

communion is more about listening."[20] Prayer is a time of heightened receptivity to God. God can speak to us through a variety of means, such as creation, Scripture, the words of others, and an inner sense of direction. As Wesley advised, what we believe to be guidance from God may need to be tested by Scripture and the Christian community. But he would also insist that prayer is one of the greatest privileges we can have, as it enables us to have genuine conversation with God.

As conversation, prayer does involve *speaking,* and many are not quite sure what to say. To this, Richard Foster has some sound advice. He reminds us that "we will never have pure enough motives, or be good enough, or know enough in order to pray rightly."[21] What we need to do is begin. God will accept our prayers and us as we are.

Foster suggests we start with the form of prayer we encounter most frequently in Scripture, which he calls "Simple Prayer." This is where "we simply and unpretentiously share our concerns and make our petitions."[22] The focus is on our needs and concerns, and, just as we do with the requests of our children, we trust God to sort out our mixed motives and confused desires, then answer us with wisdom and love.

I began this chapter with the claim that, at its heart, prayer is a desire to be in God's presence, and petition is grounded in thanksgiving and praise. It might seem that Foster's recommending "Simple Prayer" is contradicting this. But remember, Foster is trying to tell us how to begin. If we do, he believes we will slowly but surely undergo a transformation of our hearts, where "God moves from the periphery of our prayer experience to the center."[23] In Wesley's language, even the simple prayer of petition will be a means of grace.

Having made a beginning, how can we grow in our prayer life? One way is, whenever possible, to *be specific.* When we give God thanks, we are to name clearly that for which we are thankful. It is, of course, specific enough to give thanks for such major acts of God as the gift of life or this wonderful creation, the forgiveness of our sins and a new life of love. But when we thank God for "all our many blessings," it is good to specify what some of those blessings are. Likewise, our intercessions can often be more specific, especially when we are not praying for an individual. While it is good to pray for peace in the world, we can intercede more specifically for peace in Northern Ireland or the Middle East, and even more specifically for upcoming negotiations.

Our petitions can often be more specific as well. We are usually better at this when we request healing of the body than when we are praying for spiritual health. Asking God to help us grow in faith or patience or to deal with our despair or bitterness is more focused than asking God to make us a better person. The same can be said of our prayers of confession. It may be uncomfortable at times, but naming those things for which we seek forgiveness is a major aid to spiritual growth.

In fact, being specific in all forms of prayer helps us to grow as Christians because it focuses our desires on particular outcomes and makes us more receptive to God's work in our lives. It also focuses our attention, which helps counteract the natural tendency of our minds to wander during prayer.

Another way we can develop a richer prayer life is to *pray the prayers of the church*. These are the prayers that have been passed down to us by the church because of their spiritual depth and faithfulness to Christ. Many of these can be found in *The United Methodist Hymnal* and *The United Methodist Book of Worship*, as well as in other collections of prayers. The Psalms and other parts of Scripture offer rich resources for prayer, as do many hymns. The key is not simply saying them but praying them.

Of course, the most famous historic prayer is the one Jesus taught his disciples. For two thousand years, the Lord's Prayer has not only taught Christians to pray but also brought them closer to God. Taking time to reflect on this prayer in all its depth greatly strengthens our Christian lives. There are a number of good resources to help our study of this greatest of all prayers.[24]

Even those most experienced in prayer will tell of "dry" periods when God seems silent or praying seems too hard. They would urge us to *pray even when we don't feel like praying*. Wesley advised one correspondent that it is "wisdom to force ourselves to prayer; to pray whether we can pray or not."[25] Prayer is dependent not on our feelings but on our need to be in relationship with God. Praying only when we feel like it would risk breaking that relationship. It also gets us out of the habit of praying and, like any other practice, will make it harder to begin anew.

Spiritual writers who urge us to *persist* in prayer often point to Jesus' parable about a widow who through persistence wore down an unjust judge and succeeded in getting him to grant her request for justice (Luke 18:1-8). Assuring his disciples that our loving God will readily grant justice to those "who cry to him day and night" (v. 7), Jesus told this parable to show "their need to pray always and not to lose heart" (v. 1). The timing of an answer to our petitions and intercessions belongs to God, but sometimes we find our own desire for the requests we make is deepened and, as a result, our own hearts changed by our persistence in prayer.

As we have seen, Wesley is one of many who have tried to take seriously our need to *pray without ceasing*. He developed the habit of saying a short, one-sentence prayer of praise on the hour, followed by a few minutes of meditation. This enabled Wesley to bring "the events of his life before God."[26]

Steve Harper suggests taping prayer reminders to the telephone so we can pray for whoever gives us a call or placing reminders to pray throughout the house.[27] We can develop the habit of offering silent prayer for everyone we meet or every appointment on our calendars. I know of people who when caught in a traffic jam pray for those in accidents or facing frustration due to the delay.

No doubt many of us will develop other creative ways to encourage prayer. But the most important thing is for us to begin. Our need is great, and we have a God who longs for us to come home.

Discussion Questions

1. How would you describe the purpose of prayer?

2. In what ways do thanksgiving and praise, petition and confession open our lives to be changed by God?

3. Why is intercessory prayer important? How can we expand our vision of what we bring before God in prayer?

4. Why do you believe it is so difficult to pray regularly? What keeps you from praying regularly?

5. How can we be better listeners and speakers in our prayer conversation with God?

Chapter 4

The Second Practice: Scripture

I WAS HAVING a conversation with a seminary student who was telling me how much he had benefited from his Bible classes. By learning something of the original languages as well as biblical history and culture, he understood Scripture much better. He had also learned to see passages in context and to identify the points each biblical writer was making. He was pleased that some wrong interpretations on his part were now corrected.

But as much as he appreciated all of this, he also had a deep sense of loss. "The Bible," he said, "no longer speaks to me like it used to." Before coming to seminary he would pray, read a passage of Scripture, and try to hear what God was saying to him. Now armed with new knowledge, Bible dictionaries, commentaries, and the like, he would analyze Scripture, seeking to interpret it for teaching or preaching.

I learned an important lesson from that conversation: There is more than one good way to read the Bible. We need to draw upon the work of scholars to help us interpret Scripture more accurately. But even more, we need to read it prayerfully, listening for God to speak.

We see both of these ways of reading in the ministry of John Wesley. When he wrote his commentaries on the Old and New Testaments, he drew upon the best scholarship of his day. Accurate interpretation was crucial to Wesley for, as Albert Outler notes, "Scripture would be his court of first and last resort in faith and morals."[1] Scripture was the primary, governing source for Wesley's theology, the ultimate criterion by which it and all theologies must be tested.

The purpose of Wesley's theological reflection was not to get all his concepts right as an end in itself, but rather to point people to God and to the life God promises and offers. Wesley's teaching shaped the lives of its hearers by telling them how to have a relationship with God and the direction God is enabling them to grow.

But Scripture did not just govern Wesley's teaching; it shaped his entire life. Each year Wesley read through the Old Testament once and the New Testament several times. Because he was immersed in Scripture, it was interwoven in his thought and speech, as even the briefest examination of his sermons will attest. Commenting on St. Paul's exhortation to "let the word of Christ dwell in you richly" (Col. 3:16), Wesley notes that this does not mean for Scripture "to make a short stay, or an occasional visit, but take up its stated residence," and that in "the largest measure . . . so as to fill and govern the whole soul."[2] This he would wish for each of us, and of this his own life was a witness.

Two Kinds of Reading

Recently I have heard advertising for both cable television programs and newspapers aimed specifically at persons in business and finance. These claims are all alike: If you watch this program or read this newspaper, you will have the information necessary to make intelligent decisions during the day. The often-implied corollary is that if you don't, your competitors will, and they will have the information you lack.

There are two characteristics of this kind of reading and listening that we should note. The first is that its goal is to gain information. It seeks to acquire knowledge of fact and opinion that one does not already possess. The second is that it is functional. The purpose of this information is not to fulfill a desire for knowledge as an end in itself but as a means to another, very different end, namely, making money. Knowledge is valued because it is useful.

We can, of course, read the Bible in this way. Perhaps we are fascinated by ancient Near Eastern history and culture and find the Bible a welcome resource. Or we may look to Scripture for principles we can use to accomplish our vocational goals, to raise a family, or to have a good marriage. In our culture, this would be a natural way to read Scripture, which, if we interpret it well, may help us reach our goals.

But that is also the problem with informational and functional reading—we do it to reach *our* goals. We look up the difficult words, read the commentaries, examine the context, and ponder the meaning, all to gain more and hopefully useful information. The Bible is passive in the process, while our reasoning does all the work.

When we read Scripture devotionally, we reverse this process. We approach Scripture prayerfully, not trying to analyze a verse or passage but listening for God to speak to us through it. Instead of the Bible being open to our examination, we open our lives and hearts to God's examination. As Marjorie Thompson has said, our intent is "to open ourselves to how God may be speaking to us in and through any particular text."[3]

Robert Mulholland identifies two important characteristics of devotional reading. First, it is *formational*, not informational. The goal "is not to cover as much as quickly as possible" but to take time to really listen to a passage, "to allow the passage to open out to you its deeper dynamics, its multiple layers of meaning." We allow time for God to truly encounter us through the text. As a result, we do not make "the text . . . an object we control and manipulate according to our own insight and purposes." Instead, "we are the object that is shaped by the text." Thus "we come to the text with an openness to hear, to receive, to respond."[4] When Wesley describes searching the Scriptures as a means of grace, he is recognizing the role of devotional reading in forming Christian lives.

Second, Mulholland describes devotional reading as *relational* rather than functional. As we have seen, our culture tempts us to approach everything in functional terms. We could see devotional reading as a kind of technique we use to improve our lives. But like all means of grace, devotional reading is not a tool we use but a way of opening ourselves to a transforming relationship with God. Our "being shaped by the Word of God," says Mulholland, "is not something we do by our own efforts (functional); it is what God does in us when we are in a loving, receptive, responsive *relationship* with God."[5]

Mulholland reminds us that a functional reading of Scripture is not wrong—after all, Scripture can offer us sound guidance as to what we are to do. Rather, a functional reading is appropriate only as it flows out of a relationship with God.[6] To turn it around and try to root the relational in the functional is to run the risk of formalism, that "going-through-the-religious-motions" that Wesley warns about. It can even turn into asking what is the minimum we need to do to qualify for salvation. The functional approach then sees Christianity as a checklist of duties instead of a relationship of love.

We will need to look more closely at how we can have this relationship through devotional reading. But first I want to say something about the nature of Scripture itself and why it serves so well as a means of relationship with God.

The Nature of Scripture

A Bible study was examining one of Jesus' parables when two members of the group each offered different interpretations of its meaning. One then asked the pastor which of the two interpretations was correct. The assumption behind the question, shared by almost everyone in the group, was there could be only one true meaning to a parable or any other passage of Scripture. They saw the task of Bible study to uncover that meaning. It would therefore be possible for both interpretations to be wrong but not for both to be right.

Had this Bible study consisted of people from a younger generation, the assumption would likely be different. The goal would not be to discover a single objective meaning but to report what the passage "says" to each participant. There could be many, even conflicting interpretations, all accepted as valid.

I find the first approach to be overly narrow but the second far too wide. A passage of Scripture cannot mean anything we want it to mean—there are, after all, wrong interpretations. Yet it often means more than we think. In fact, it can have a multiplicity of meanings.

The Bible contains a variety of kinds of literature: psalms, proverbs, prophets, letters, but above all narratives. For the most part, this is not the sort of literature that has a single, precise meaning. A narrative especially resists neat summaries that claim to say what the story means. If a friend offers to tell you the meaning of a story so you won't have to go to the trouble of reading it for yourself, you would be wise to beware. For if you read the story yourself, you might justifiably protest that there is so much more in it than your friend summarizes.

Stories show how characters and plot interweave over time.[7] The Bible, for all its diverse components, can be seen as a single story, beginning with creation and culminating

47

with a new heaven and earth, telling all that God has done in creation and redemption. Scripture shows us our world from God's perspective, which is very different from our normal way of looking at things. It tells us who we were created to be, provides a diagnosis of our problem, and shows what God is doing to bring us and our world new life.

As it presents how God is at work in the world, Scripture reveals the character of God. We come to know who God is from what God has done, is doing, and has promised. Most especially, we learn who God is through the stories of Jesus Christ. It is the life and death of Jesus that more than anything reveals what we mean when we say God is love.

So far, what we've said about Scripture could also be said about a good novel—it tells a story that pictures a world and shows the character of the people in it by their interaction with circumstances and one another. As in a novel, we come to know the various characters in the Bible such as Abraham, Sarah, Moses, David, Elijah, Mary, Peter, and Paul by following their stories.

But besides its multiple human authorship and diverse literature, the Bible is different from a novel in two other important ways. First, Scripture tells of God's involvement in history, even personally entering our history in Jesus Christ. Although the Bible is rich in imagery, the realities of which it speaks are far from imaginary. This is an account of the living God who actually created our world and in whose hands rests our future. This is the God who in Christ forgives our sins and through the Spirit gives us new life. When we enter the world of the Bible, we find a God who is very much involved in our world.

Second, Scripture is a means of grace through which the Holy Spirit transforms our lives. If the Bible were more like an encyclopedia or a self-help book, then we would use it as a tool to help us improve our lives or reach our goals. But the Bible is full of stories, images, parables, psalms, letters, and the like that elude our control. They always mean more than we can say. We can return to them again and again, each time seeing something that we had missed before. Scripture is therefore an ideal tool of the Spirit to enable us to grow in the knowledge and love of God. The Spirit can speak God's word to us afresh, applying it to our lives and world. As we encounter God through the Spirit while reading Scripture, we come to know God more fully, and our love for God and neighbor grows as a result.

A devotional reading of Scripture opens us to an encounter with God in which we hear God speak to our hearts and lives. It is, along with prayer and the sacraments, the most important way we remain in a relationship with God. We can now look in more detail at how we can enter into a devotional reading of Scripture.

Searching the Scriptures

Wesley offers his advice for the devotional reading of Scripture by asking a series of questions. Do we "search the Scriptures" by

(1) Reading: Constantly, some part of every day; regularly, all the Bible in order; carefully, with the Notes; seriously, with prayer before and after; fruitfully, immediately practising what you learn there?

(2) Meditating: At set times? by any rule?[8]

This approach is itself rooted in a more ancient method called *lectio divina*, or "sacred reading." It is a four-part process consisting of reflective reading, meditation as an active interaction with the text and on how it relates to our lives, prayer in response, and contemplation as a resting in the experience, a trusting that God's word will be effective and an openness to follow where it leads. There are a number of good resources that can provide guidance for those wishing to engage in devotional reading through *lectio divina*.[9] Here I will elaborate on Wesley's advice, drawing on some of my earlier research as well as the insights of Robert Mulholland.[10]

"Constantly" has to do with the time we devote to devotional reading. Wesley suggests each of us "set apart a little time, if you can, every morning and evening for that purpose."[11] Certainly we should do this once a day at least. Mulholland notes that this time should be "unhindered," free from outward interruptions as well as a time when we can let go of the pressures, the problems, the burdens of our daily lives.[12] We also need to find a location that is not so distracting or uncomfortable as to interfere with our devotional reading.

By "regularly," Wesley advises we "read a chapter out of the Old, and one out of the New, Testament"; if this is not possible, then "take a single chapter, or a part of one."[13] In this way we will read the entire Bible through again and again. Others suggest using the lectionary as a source for daily Scripture readings. It is helpful to have a plan that will enable you to read all or most of the Bible over time.

To read "carefully" is to remind us how each passage fits within the whole of Scripture. Wesley was convinced that Scripture had central themes, such as God's love and the story of creation, fall, and salvation, that gave it an overarching unity. His *Notes* on the two testaments were designed to assist readers in keeping these larger themes in mind.

To read "seriously" is to surround our devotional reading with prayer. When we read Scripture devotionally, we read it in the presence of God. Therefore

> serious and earnest prayer should be constantly used before we consult the oracles of God, seeing "Scripture can only be understood through the same Spirit whereby it was given." Our reading should likewise be closed with prayer, that what we read may be written on our hearts.[14]

Prayer, along with an unhurried silence, is essential for us to enter into God's presence in a way that we can then hear God's word. Marjorie Thompson compares the resulting attentiveness with how one reads a love letter, allowing "the words that are pregnant and weighty with meaning to sink in and expand and nourish your heart." Each sentence of Scripture is read "as if for the first time, expecting that God will address you with a direct and personal message."[15]

"Meditating," says Wesley, involves our taking the time to reflect on what we have read "with all the attention and earnestness of which" the "mind is capable."[16] What is God saying to us in this passage? What in our reading seems especially striking, or comforting, or challenging, or convicting? What implications does this have for how we live—our values, commitments, relationships, and activities?

Wesley believed it useful "frequently to pause, and examine ourselves by what we read, both with regard to our hearts and lives." Through meditation we may find that God has "enabled us to conform to his blessed will," which elicits our praise; we may become "conscious of having fallen short," evoking prayer and humility. But "whatever light you then receive should be used to the uttermost, and that immediately."[17] To do this is to read Scripture "fruitfully," putting into practice whatever God has shown us.

Many long to hear a word from God. When we come to Scripture with an expectant faith, taking the time to really listen, we give God an opportunity to say a word that can transform our lives. To be open and receptive to the Holy Spirit and to read, as Wesley said, with a desire "to know the whole will of God, and a fixed resolution to do it,"[18] is to enter into a relationship that may at times be challenging but will unquestionably be fulfilling. We will find ourselves touched again and again by God's gracious love in Christ and increasingly shaped into persons whose hearts and lives reflect that love to the world.

Discussion Questions

1. How do you usually read the Bible? Do you use study aids such as Bible dictionaries, concordances, and commentaries? Do you begin with prayer and listen for God to speak? How have you found your approach helpful?

2. Contrast reading the Bible for information and for formation. What are the advantages and disadvantages of each?

3. Contrast reading the Bible functionally and relationally. What are the strengths of each? Which do you think has priority and why?

4. Think of the different kinds of literature in the Bible. How do you think we should read each kind? For instance, should we read a gospel differently from one of Paul's letters or a psalm differently from a prophet like Jeremiah? How should we read a parable? a proverb?

5. What do you see as the value of meditating on Scripture? How would you go about it?

Chapter 5

The Third Practice: Word and Table

I DIDN'T GET anything out of that service!" Perhaps you have made a comment something like this or at least thought it. I have heard it said many times. It may indicate a failed expectation; all too often it simply acknowledges that once again worship somehow was disappointing.

The problem is not just a modern one. In Wesley's day, there were many who were alienated from the worship of the Church of England. Some of the complaints were legitimate. Sermons could be so learned or filled with allusions to classical literature that they were over the heads of everyday people. The singing, which consisted of lining the Psalms,[1] was often less than inspiring. For many, worship seemed unconnected to everyday life.

Wesley's response to this was interesting. On the one hand, he pioneered new forms of worship, especially within the Methodist societies. He sought to preach "plain truth for plain people," abstaining "as far as possible from even the show of learning."[2] He published his brother's hymns, igniting a revolution in lively singing. He borrowed covenant services from the Puritans and love feasts from the Moravian Bretheren. In all of this, his goal was to foster participation in worship by the people called Methodist.

On the other hand, he was quick to defend the liturgy of the Church of England. To complaints that the Methodists did not get "fed" at the church services, Wesley responded:

> If it be said, 'But at the Church we are fed with chaff, whereas at the Meeting we have wholesome food,' we answer: (1) The Prayers of the Church are not chaff—they are substantial food for any who are alive to God. (2) The Lord's Supper is not chaff, but pure and wholesome for all who receive it with upright hearts. Yea, (3) in almost all the sermons we hear there we hear many great and important truths.[3]

Wesley insists that how we experience worship depends greatly on how we approach worship: "alive to God," "with upright hearts." To put this differently, what makes worship meaningful is whether we come with expectant faith, an openness to the presence and power of God.

Probably most of the readers of this book are not directly involved in planning worship, but almost all of us regularly attend worship. But being in attendance is not the same as actually worshiping. Wesley gives us two important clues for strengthening our involvement in worship.

First, we cannot worship if we are simply an audience or a group of spectators. Worship necessarily requires *participation*; it is something we do. As Robert Webber says, "Worship is a verb."[4]

Second, we close ourselves off from worship if we do not expect anything is going to happen. For us to worship, we need a sense of *expectancy*—we come expecting to meet God, to be in God's presence, give God praise, hear God speak, respond to God's call, and be touched by God's grace. We expect that as a result, our lives will be different from having worshiped God. To come with a desire for God and even a slight degree of faith can transform worship from a meaningless routine to a means of grace.

What Is Worship

Jesus told the woman of Samaria that "true worshipers will worship the Father in spirit and truth, for the Father seeks such as these to worship him" (John 4:23). Sally Morgenthaler finds that many contemporary definitions of worship gravitate toward either "spirit" or "truth," and there is much to learn from each.[5] She gives two examples, which I will cite along with comments of my own.

For the first, she draws upon Gerrit Gustafson, who defines worshiping in "spirit" as "the act and attitude of wholeheartedly giving ourselves to God, spirit, soul and body. Worship is simply the expression of our love for God."[6] This understands true worship to flow out of a *right heart* (one directed to God) and lead to acts of praise and self-offering.

Worshiping in "truth" is described by Robert Webber when he says, "Worship celebrates God's saving deed in Jesus Christ."[7] Here, worship is fundamentally a *right remembering* of what God has done in Christ as the reason for our praise and thanksgiving. That is, Christian worship is at its heart a celebration of the victory won by God over sin, suffering, injustice, and death, and for the new life given to us and offered to all through Jesus Christ.

As I have said elsewhere, this "remembering" means much more than recalling to mind "a past event or person that is no longer present." In biblical remembrance, the past "event or person becomes present to us—it is something like experiencing that event or person anew, as a present reality."[8]

The Jewish Passover, in which the events of the Exodus are remembered, is an example of this. The Exodus is an event in the past. But in the Passover, as Don Saliers has said, "It is clear also that on the *present* night—in this very prayer and ritual action of the meal—the liberating power of that past event is here and now, made actual among the community of memory and hope."[9]

The same could be said of Christian celebrations of the Lord's Supper and hearing the Word read and proclaimed.

Here is the central point: it is as we remember rightly through our participation in worship that the Spirit of God gives us right hearts. And it is as we come to worship with hearts seeking God that we remember rightly. Through this dynamic of right heart and right remembrance, spirit, and truth, we grow in the knowledge and love of God and in love for our neighbor.

Now let's look at worship from a slightly different angle. James F. White, among many others, describes the central purpose of worship to be "the glorification of God and the sanctification of humanity."[10] Our heartfelt desire for God and our remembrance of God's acts of salvation combine to enable us to glorify God through praise, thanksgiving, and service. As we glorify God in this way, we are sanctified, growing in the Christian life.

This only happens if our worship is centered on God. All too often services of worship take on other, more human-centered goals. We can place the focus on celebrating our own accomplishments or use the service to enlist participation in church programs. While these may be good, we should beware of letting them push God out of the center of our worship. Worship that does not glorify God does not sanctify as well—it cannot serve as a means of grace.

We have discussed worship as something we do. But it is vital to see worship as an event in which God is active as well. Worship, says Morgenthaler, is a "two-way communication between believers and God, a dialogue of response involving both actions and speech."[11] A service of worship is structured something like a dialogue in which, in Webber's words, "God speaks and acts," and the people "respond through word and deed."[12] The central way God speaks is through Scripture and preaching; the central way God acts is through the Lord's Supper.

Hearing and Responding to God's Word

Our participation in worship is enhanced when we see how it is patterned. The basic pattern of worship used in many United Methodist churches today has a fourfold structure: Entrance, Proclamation and Response, Thanksgiving and Communion, and the Sending Forth.[13] The centrality of the two middle parts of this structure has led this to be called a "Word and Table" pattern.

This basic pattern is rooted in the practice of the earliest Christians, reflecting the New Testament witness as well as other ancient Christian writings from as early as the second century. It can be seen in the story of the two disciples on the road to Emmaus in Luke 24. They had seen Jesus crucified, and their hope "that he was the one to redeem Israel" (v. 21) had been crushed. There were rumors that the tomb was empty and Jesus was alive, but they did not know what to make of such stories.

They were joined on their journey by Jesus, whom they did not recognize. His first act was to proclaim the *word*: "Then beginning with Moses and all the prophets, he interpreted to them the things about himself in all the scriptures" (v. 27). When they stopped to stay overnight at a village, his second act was at the *table* when "he took bread, blessed and broke it, and gave it to them" (v. 30). It was then that they recognized him. Jesus disappeared, but they rushed back to Jerusalem that same evening to share the good news—one of the most remarkable "Sending Forths" in church history.

While many local churches follow this word and table pattern, they may have very different services of worship. But whatever their order of worship, each service is bound to include Scripture, a sermon, prayers, hymns, and perhaps other elements such as doxologies, affirmations of faith, and invitations. In fact, it would be impossible to have worship at all without at least the reading of Scripture and prayer.

We come to worship with many things on our minds. Some of the distractions may be trivial—snatches of a song we heard or images from a television commercial. Others may be of great significance—financial difficulties, a friend with marital problems, a child in trouble, a spouse facing surgery. We need not be concerned about our minds wandering as we begin our worship due to these many thoughts. In fact, given the busyness of many of our lives, it is a welcome luxury just to have a moment to think on them. It is important that we bring all this with us to worship, for how else can we lay these concerns before God?

When the service begins, it is often by our offering praise and thanksgiving to God through singing hymns or other kinds of "praise songs." This way of starting our worship has a long lineage:

> Make a joyful noise to the LORD,
>   all the earth.
> Worship the Lord with gladness;
> come into his presence with singing. . . .
>
> Enter his gates with thanksgiving,
>   and his courts with praise.
> Give thanks to him, bless his name. (Ps. 100:1-2, 4)

Beginning with praise and thanksgiving is a way for us to turn our thoughts to God and enter into God's presence.

The heart of the service of the word is the reading of Scripture. To say this may seem odd because we are used to thinking of the sermon as the central element. But even more than the sermon, the Scripture passages determine a theme or set of themes for the service, which the sermon then takes and develops for our lives and world today. In fact, in a well-planned service, the hymns, prayers, and other parts of worship all at least loosely revolve around these scriptural themes.

My kindergarten teacher often said, "If you listen, you will hear." I try to keep this in mind whenever Scripture is read aloud in worship. As we hear the words of Scripture, the Holy Spirit will speak to receptive hearts, sometimes in surprising ways. Even before we hear the sermon, we may find ourselves comforted or challenged, assured or unsettled, receiving needed guidance or facing new questions as we listen to God's word in Scripture.

It is the task of the sermon to proclaim God's word to contemporary hearers. In order to proclaim God's word faithfully, the sermon should be based in Scripture; in order to speak to today, it must address our lives, culture, and world.

Sermons can take a variety of forms. Some begin with Scripture and move to present-day concerns; others start with a contemporary question or issue and then move to Scripture. Topics can range from how to pray to how to love and serve our neighbor, from building family relationships to current social issues. The hope is that all sermons will proclaim the good news of what God has done in the life, death, and resurrection of Jesus Christ and what God is doing through the Holy Spirit.

Besides discerning the "shape" of the sermon, there are two other ways we can become better listeners. If the scriptural texts for the next Sunday are known in advance, then we can study them ahead of time, perhaps incorporating them into our daily devotions. For some, this practice has made an enormous difference in how they hear sermons.

Another way to focus our listening is to seek to identify what a sermon is asking us to do. A sermon could be inviting us to give any of a number of responses—to have faith, give thanks, confess our sin, grow as Christians, or make a fresh commitment. The best sermons in my opinion make the invitation explicit, letting it flow naturally out of the message, and provide a concrete way for hearers to respond. But almost all sermons are implicitly invitational.

Other acts of worship such as hymns, prayers of confession and intercession, and affirmations of faith are responses to God's word and presence. These acts of worship we do together as the people of God. We share a faith that has been passed on to us by others, we confess our sins as a community, and we cry out to God together for our common concerns.

Hymns can be especially powerful means of grace if we attend to what we are singing. Hymns can be testimonies ("Amazing grace! How sweet the sound that saved a wretch like me!"), proclamation ("Christ the Lord is risen today"), or invitations ("Come, sinners, to the gospel feast"). Notice that these hymns are sung to each other and to the world. Other hymns are prayers of praise ("Holy, holy, holy!"), confession ("Just as I am, without one plea"), consecration ("Take my life, and let it be consecrated, Lord, to thee"), or requests for sanctification and empowerment ("Love divine, all loves excelling"; "Spirit of the living God, fall afresh on me"). These, as prayers, are sung to God.

Because worship is communal, it can provide support amid the many distractions and concerns of life. As Robert Mulholland says, "When we don't feel like worshiping, the community should carry us along in its worship."[14] Perhaps we just can't seem to pray or our faith is weak. Others in the community continue to pray, read Scripture, and affirm the faith of the church, helping us through the strength of their faith. On another day it will be our faith that lends support to someone next to us as we worship God together.

Worship is not a temporary escape from the cares of this world. In fact, in the words of Don Saliers, it is only when our praise, confession, and intercession speak to "our actual suffering and rejoicing, our hopes and fears" that worship is both "true and relevant."[15] Rather than setting aside the concerns we bring with us, we set them before God. Vital worship will address the concerns we bring as well as lift before us the concerns of God. At its best, worship enables us to look at our lives and our world afresh as seen by the eyes of God.

Coming to the Lord's Table

If the word is the heart of worship, the table is its goal. Worship culminates in a profound thanksgiving for God's victory over sin and death, gift of new life, and communion together with the risen Christ at his table. Because of this, John and Charles Wesley, like Martin Luther and John Calvin before them, would have us restore the New Testament church practice of celebrating the Lord's Supper weekly. Many United Methodist churches today have at least moved toward Wesley's ideal of "constant communion" by celebrating it monthly.

The desire of the early Methodists to receive the Lord's Supper as often as possible is well known. The enormous crowds of communicants would sometimes take hours to serve. Why this hunger for the sacrament? They were convinced that, through the power of the Holy Spirit, the risen Jesus Christ was present in this meal, and by receiving his gifts of bread and wine, they would be given new life. They came with an expectant faith, seeking to remember all that God has done and promised through Jesus Christ and open to receive all God has to give.

As with worship in general, our own participation can be enhanced and expectancy heightened by seeing the pattern of the Lord's Supper. It is based on Jesus' actions during the Last Supper as recounted in the New Testament (Matt. 26:26-29, Mark 14:22-25, Luke 22:19-20, 1 Cor. 11:23-26). Jesus first takes the bread, then blesses it (or gives thanks), breaks the bread, and gives it to the disciples. Likewise, he takes the cup, gives thanks, and gives it to the disciples.

The service in *The United Methodist Hymnal*[16] is organized around these four simple actions:

THANKSGIVING
1. Taking the bread and cup
2. The prayer of Great Thanksgiving
COMMUNION
3. Breaking the bread
4. Giving the bread and cup

The pairing of these four actions shows the appropriateness of other common names for the Lord's Supper. Eucharist means "thanksgiving," while Holy Communion is linked to our communion with Christ and one another as we share the bread and the cup.

At the beginning of the meal, the bread and wine (which for most United Methodists is grape juice) either are brought to the table during the offering or have already been placed on the table. The celebrant (usually the pastor) *takes* the bread and wine and prepares them for the meal. If one or more large cups (or chalices) are being used in the service, the pastor may pour wine from a pitcher into them at this time.

Then the celebrant gives *thanks*, offering a prayer of Great Thanksgiving. This may be one of the prayers in the hymnal or *The United Methodist Book of Worship*, or a prayer either composed in advance or prayed extemporaneously. Our eucharistic prayers today are shaped much like the Great Thanksgivings that were prayed during the early centuries of Christian worship.

If you examine a prayer of Great Thanksgiving, you will find it tells the story of God's involvement with the world from creation to the coming kingdom and organizes that story around the three persons of the Trinity. The prayer begins by remembering God's goodness to creation and to Israel as well as acknowledging human sin. It then relates how God has saved us through Jesus Christ and includes the "words of institution" spoken by Jesus at his last supper with his disciples before his death. We then offer ourselves to Christ in response to his giving himself for us. The prayer culminates in a call for the Holy Spirit to be poured out on us and the gifts of bread and wine, and with a joyful anticipation of Christ's coming again in final victory.

We see here the significance of remembrance. As this prayer is prayed, we experience anew God's infinite love and wonderful salvation through Jesus Christ. We remember in order to give thanks, and it is as we give thanks that the Holy Spirit continues to draw us ever closer to God and to one another. The dominant mood is thus one of joy and praise, a celebration of God's great victory over sin, suffering, and death through the resurrection of Jesus Christ.

At the conclusion of the Great Thanksgiving, we often pray the Lord's Prayer. Then the celebrant *breaks* the bread and servers *give* the bread and wine to the congregation. Sometimes this is done as people are kneeling at the altar rail; at other times, they receive standing (as was common among the earliest Christians who saw it as a sign of resurrection). Sometimes people will serve each other while seated in a circle or at a table. If a chalice (or "common cup") is used, the bread and wine are often received by intinction, that is, by dipping a piece of bread into the cup.

Whatever the method, the promise of the sacrament is the same: Through the power of the Holy Spirit, the risen Jesus is present at this meal, giving us these gifts of bread and wine. And, in giving these gifts, Jesus gives himself in love, offering forgiveness and new life. As we partake of this meal, we receive in us the life of God and increasingly reflect in our own lives the love that is in Jesus Christ.

Discussion Questions

1. What kinds of expectations do you bring to a service of worship? How do our expectations affect our participation?

2. In what ways does God speak to us in worship? How can we become better listeners?

3. What are some of the ways we respond to God through our worship?

4. How is remembering as "experiencing anew" different from "recalling to mind"?

5. Think about gifts you have received. Is there a way in which, in giving the gift, the giver has given something of himself or herself? How is this similar and different from the gifts of bread and wine Christ gives to us in the Lord's Supper?

Our Common Life

We share that a commitment to Jesus Christ manifests itself in a common heart and life, binding believers together in a common fellowship and anticipating solidarity within the human family.

- Having experienced the Gospel of Jesus Christ as a liberating power from all oppression, we stand in solidarity with all people who seek freedom, peace, and justice.

- Knowing that the love we share in Christ is stronger than our conflicts, broader than our opinions, and deeper than the wounds we inflict on one another, we commit ourselves to participation in our congregations, denominations, and the whole Christian family for the purpose of nurture, outreach, and witness.

- Remembering our gospel commitment to "love our neighbors," we will, through dialogue and partnerships for service to the world, endeavor to establish relationships with believers of other world traditions.

Adopted by the World Methodist Council
Rio de Janeiro, August 13, 1996

Community United Methodist Church
1548 South Hart Street Road
Vincennes, Indiana 47591
Office # (812) 882-2220 FAX# (812) 882-4255
http://www.Community-UMC.org

Chapter 6

The Fourth Practice: Renewal and Healing

THERE IS A rhythm to worship. The most basic is our weekly pattern of coming together to worship, usually on Sunday. In the New Testament, this is called the Lord's Day, the day of the Resurrection. Today churches with multiple weekly services sometimes schedule them on other days, most often Saturday evening.

Another rhythm, followed by John Wesley, is the practice of daily worship, in which people come together for morning and evening prayer. Even more familiar to United Methodist churches is the annual pattern of the liturgical year. It tells the story of Jesus, with one cycle starting with Advent and moving to Christmas and Epiphany; and a second beginning with Ash Wednesday and Lent, moving to Palm/Passion Sunday, Maundy Thursday, and Good Friday; and then culminating in Easter and Pentecost. Celebrating the church year is yet another way to remember and give thanks for all that God has done through Jesus Christ and the Holy Spirit.

Early Methodists had other rhythms of worship. One was the annual service in which they renewed their covenant with God. Another was worship at the quarterly society meetings in which the love feasts were held. In this chapter, I want to discuss these two forms of worship, along with services recovering Wesley's practice of prayer for healing. In addition, I will show how Wesley's service of covenant renewal is linked to our contemporary services in which we renew our Baptismal Covenant.

While all of these forms of worship have past, present, and future dimensions, it does seem to me that the emphasis is different for each. Baptism and covenant renewal look back, remembering and giving thanks for what God has done. Love feasts focus on the present, giving testimony to what God is doing now. Healing services look with hope and anticipation for what God may yet do in our lives and world. In all of these, God is at the center of our worship, and as we give God thanks and praise, these services become means of grace for our lives.

Renewing Our Covenant

On August 11, 1755, Methodists held their first Covenant Service. Drawn from the writings of Puritan Richard Alleine, the service involved hearing the promises of God, giving God thanks for guarding and guiding God's people, and then, in response to God's faithfulness, renewing the people's commitment to love and serve God. "After I had recited the tenor of the covenant proposal," reported Wesley, ". . . all the people stood up, in testimony of assent, to the number of about eighteen hundred persons. Such a night I scarce ever saw before. Surely the fruit of it shall remain for ever."[1]

The practice of covenant renewal spread throughout early Methodism. In London it became common to hold Covenant Services on New Year's Day; elsewhere they were held as occasional services led by John Wesley. While Wesley's service consisted mostly of the people listening and then assenting, later versions provided for more congregational participation throughout the service. A contemporary version of a Covenant Renewal Service is found in *The United Methodist Book of Worship*.[2]

Although baptism is directly mentioned only once in Wesley's Covenant Service, clearly it is the Baptismal Covenant that is being renewed. Because God is faithful and has no need to renew the Baptismal Covenant, the service gives thanks for God's faithfulness. However, though we professed our faith in baptism, we are not always faithful. We need from time to time to turn our hearts to God by renewing our promise to follow Christ, and the Covenant Service enables us to do this.[3]

While many United Methodist churches today use a Wesleyan Covenant Service, many others are adopting a more recent service for the same purpose. This is the congregational reaffirmation of the Baptismal Covenant found in *The United Methodist Hymnal*.[4] The most significant difference between this service and a Covenant Service is that it for the most part follows the same pattern and contains the same words as a service of baptism. The strength of this service is it enables participants to experience anew (remember) all that God has done in and through their baptism and to reaffirm their commitment in response.

In baptism, we are initiated into the life of the church and incorporated into God's acts of salvation in Jesus Christ. Through our entering into this new community with its means of grace and receiving our new identity in Christ, we are given a new life and enabled to live it out faithfully.[5] We remember this gracious gift of God when we reaffirm our baptismal vows.

The order of the service is much like baptism itself. We begin by publicly renouncing sin and professing our faith, committing ourselves to the same promises made in baptism. Then, as Christians did during the early centuries of the church, we affirm our belief in the Apostles' Creed in response to three historic questions, one for each person of the Trinity.

These acts of professing our faith are followed by a prayer of thanksgiving that remembers and narrates the story of salvation. Like the Great Thanksgiving in the Lord's Supper, this prayer narrates the story around the three persons of the Trinity. The difference is that it recounts God's acts of creation and redemption by drawing upon the wealth of water images in the Bible: the waters of Creation, the flood of Noah, the parting of the sea in Exodus, Jesus nurtured in a womb and baptized by John, the pouring out of the Spirit, and the washing away of our sins.

In a service of baptism, this prayer would be followed by the act of baptism itself, in which water is administered (by immersion, pouring, or sprinkling) and the pastor says, "I baptize you in the name of the Father, and of the Son, and of the Holy Spirit." Then hands are laid on the recipient, and a prayer is offered for the Holy Spirit to work within his or her life.

When we reaffirm our baptismal vows, we are not being rebaptized. Since baptism is a sacrament through which God acts, to rebaptize would question God's faithfulness to what God has already done in baptism. Thus the words "I baptize you . . ." are not repeated. Instead, we are asked to "remember your baptism and be thankful," simple words that point us to a profound truth: God through Jesus Christ has made us part of the family of God, has forgiven our sins and given us new life, and has made clear a love that is eternal. To experience this anew is to be grateful beyond words and joyously recommit our lives to Christ, who gave his life for us.

I have seen the baptismal reaffirmation service done in a variety of circumstances and water used in many different ways. Persons who have either returned to the Christian faith or experienced spiritual renewal have reaffirmed their commitment to God through this service. Youth who were baptized as infants can make their first public profession of faith in this way. Because, like Wesley, United Methodism understands baptism to be a means through which God graciously acts, we have always held as valid the baptism of infants. But because we do not view grace as irresistible, we have likewise held that salvation requires faith. The renewal of the Baptismal Covenant is highly appropriate for baptized youth who want to profess their faith as well as Christians who are returning to God.

Our focus is on those times when entire congregations reaffirm their Baptismal Covenant. While Wesley's Covenant Service is often used the first Sunday in January, local congregations who follow the Christian year frequently have services of baptismal renewal on the second Sunday, which remembers the baptism of Jesus. Other common occasions are charge conferences and annual conferences. Renewal of the Baptismal Covenant, like the Covenant Service, is appropriate on almost any occasion.

Water is used in ways that do not signify baptism. Sometimes the celebrant walks through the congregation sprinkling water and saying, "Remember your baptism and be thankful." I have seen services where a person comes forward and has the sign of the cross placed on his or her forehead with water, or the person reaches into a font or bowl of water and retrieves a shell, which is an ancient symbol of baptism.

The first time I participated in a service of baptismal reaffirmation, the congregation came forward in two lines. The pastor and I would take water from the font, put it into the hand of the person before us, look into his or her eyes, and say, "Remember your baptism and be thankful." While I believed this would be a meaningful service, I was unprepared for the powerfully positive response it elicited. Many had gone their entire lives not thinking about their baptism, much less remembering it on this deeper level. At least for that congregation it was a significant moment of renewal.

We ended the service by praying together a covenant prayer in the Wesleyan tradition. Its words express well the deep recommitment that both Wesleyan Covenant Services and the reaffirmation of our Baptismal Covenant can elicit:

> I am no longer my own, but thine.
> Put me to what thou wilt, rank me with whom thou wilt.
> Put me to doing, put me to suffering.
> Let me be employed by thee or laid aside for thee,
> exalted for thee or brought low for thee.
> Let me be full, let me be empty.
> Let me have all things, let me have nothing.
> I freely and heartily yield all things
> to thy pleasure and disposal.
> And now, O glorious and blessed God,
> Father, Son, and Holy Spirit,
> thou art mine, and I am thine. So be it.
> And the covenant which I have made on earth,
> let it be ratified in heaven. **Amen.**[6]

Sharing Our Testimony

Today many Americans eat on the run. The term *fast food* has entered our vocabulary and marks our lives. All too often family members, faced with different commitments in different places at different times, no longer sit down and have a meal together.

Jesus' ministry stands in sharp contrast with our way of eating. He too had many demands on his time. But meals were seen as special events, occasions for sharing and conversation as much as a means of physical nourishment. His meals with his disciples were times of great importance.

The early church continued the practice of having meals together as the family of God. Originally they were full meals begun by the breaking of bread and concluded by the sharing of the cup, much like Jesus' last supper with his disciples. By the first century, the full meal was dropped, and the Lord's Supper became the meal of bread and wine we know today.

From time to time, Christians have sought to recover the extended fellowship and sharing of those early meals. The Moravian love feast was one such attempt. When John Wesley first encountered a love feast in Savannah, Georgia, he was deeply impressed. They became one of the most common features of early Methodism in both England and America.

Love feasts were enormously popular. In England, they were at one time held as often as once a month; in America, they were among the highlights of the quarterly conference. Lasting about ninety minutes, they had a standard pattern of worship: hymn, prayer, a meal of bread and water, a collection for the poor, testimony, hymn, prayer, and benediction. (Americans moved the collection to the end of the service.)[7]

Wesley spoke for most Methodists when he reported, "At these *love-feasts* . . . our food is only a little plain cake and water. But we seldom return from them without being fed, not only with 'the meat which perisheth,' but with 'that which endureth to everlasting life.'"[8] At the heart of the love feast was the sharing of testimonies. Large numbers of Methodists were drawn to the love feasts to hear these testimonies.

The sharing of testimonies of what God had done in their lives was second nature to early Methodists. It was a highly participatory experience. Offering testimony required no special theological training; indeed it included those entirely without education. It was open to men and women and young and old, of all classes and races. The testimonies were an encouragement to those seeking justification, new birth, and Christian perfection, or struggling with assurance or their calling. Most of all, they were occasions to rejoice at what God was doing in the lives of others and to strengthen anticipation for what God might do in their own.

We are not used to sharing testimonies today, but I am convinced there are large numbers of United Methodists, as well as those seeking faith, who long for such experiences. Some of this is occurring in small groups. But we have an opportunity to recover the love feast as a regular part of our life together. At one church I pastored we did this—our first love feast was so popular it became a quarterly event.

There are instructions and an order for a love feast in *The United Methodist Book of Worship*.[9] Although early Methodist love feasts used bread and water, today they are celebrated with a variety of breads and beverages, though not with wine, grape juice, or bread that would imply this meal is the Lord's Supper. In our service we actually had a very simple meal—if a full meal (like a potluck) is desired, that is best held immediately after the love feast. The key is simplicity and sharing.

Early Methodist testimonies centered on experiences of justification, new birth, assurance, and Christian perfection. So many people were coming into the movement that there was no lack of fresh testimonies of this kind. These are still welcome today, especially when they are new experiences. But our love feasts might also give witness to God's comfort in times of grief, guidance in times of confusion, healing in times of illness, or empowerment to care for those in need or share the good news with our neighbors. Sharing what God is doing today confirms for all participants that God is actively at work, and it strengthens hope and faith in the goodness of God.

Hoping in a God Who Heals

In all four Gospels, healing the sick is shown to be a regular part of Jesus' ministry. According to Acts, it was central to the ministry of the apostles, and the letters of Paul and

James indicate healing was a common practice in early Christian congregations.

Our age is vastly different from that of Jesus and the first Christians. We live in a scientific age that has seen marvelous advances in medicine. People are living longer. While we still face terrible diseases such as cancer and AIDS, we have confidence that scientific research will eventually lead to cures of these and many more afflictions. In such a world as this, is healing by God credible?

John Wesley, who lived at the dawning of the age of science, would answer with an emphatic "yes!" Not that Wesley was opposed to medical science; he was in fact highly interested in advances in the cure and treatment of diseases. What concerned him was the plight of the poor who lacked the necessary funds to pay doctors and hospitals for treatment but had an abundance of illnesses and injuries.

His solution was to open dispensaries in three cities and to meet weekly with patients. Assisted by a surgeon and apothecary, Wesley would diagnose illnesses and prescribe treatments. In order to make medical knowledge available to a wider audience, in 1747 he published his *Primitive Physick: An Easy and Natural Way of Curing Most Diseases.* His most popular book, the *Primitive Physick* went through numerous editions and was in print in England and America long after Wesley's death.

In this book, Wesley offered potential cures for over 250 medical problems. He drew upon traditional folk remedies as well as the latest practices of medical science, although he avoided dangerous treatments or expensive medicines. Some of his suggestions may seem odd: To cure baldness, he suggests rubbing "the part morning and evening, with onions, till it is red; and rub it afterwards with honey."[10] He was overly enamored with the curative power of mild doses of electricity. Yet many of his suggestions would seem common sense to us; others were no different from those of the doctors of his day, and some were quite advanced. He was the first person to put into popular print this advice for assisting someone seemingly suffocated: "Blow strongly with bellows down his throat. This may recover a person seemingly drowned. It is still better if a strong man blows into his mouth."[11]

Wesley's appreciation of traditional remedies and medical science in no way dampened his belief in prayer. "God has more than one method of healing either the soul or the body,"[12] he insisted and recorded numerous instances of healing that occurred in response to prayer alone. Wesley did not pit medicine and prayer against each other but saw both as means God uses to heal.

Even when people do not have access to doctors or hospitals, they do have access to God. This is why from Wesley's day to our own, prayer for healing has been a common practice for those on the lower end of the economic scale. But today we are seeing a resurgence of interest in healing prayer that crosses all classes and cultures.

Healing services in local churches are increasingly common today. The United Methodist Book of Worship contains two services of healing plus several related services.[13] The Healing and Wholeness Ministries of the Upper Room have a number of books, seminars, and studies to aid in developing and understanding a ministry of healing.[14]

All of these resources see the Lord's Supper as itself a healing sacrament. But the distinctive element in all the services of worship is prayer for healing that is accompanied by the laying on of hands and anointing with oil. This practice is rooted in the New Testament itself: "Are any among you sick? They should call for the elders of the church and have them pray over them, anointing them with oil in the name of the Lord" (James 5:14).

As the term *wholeness* indicates, healing involves the whole person: mind, body, spirit, and relationships with God and others. This agrees with Wesley, who recognized how all of these areas of our lives mutually influence one another for good or for ill. Wholeness also means that while we may pray for one thing, God may act to heal us in another way. As James K. Wagner reminds us, "Wholeness does not necessarily mean perfect physical health." In fact, the greatest healing is our "union or reunion" with God. "When this happens," says Wagner, "physical healing sometimes occurs, mental and emotional balance is often restored. But without fail, spiritual health is enhanced and relationships are healed."[15]

There are a number of popular teachings about healing that are questionable. One of the most common turns divine healing into a formula: If you have faith that God will heal you, you will be healed. There are some passages of Scripture, especially in Mark's Gospel, that give credence to this view. But the accounts of healing in the Bible do not have a single pattern. Certainly expectant faith is an important factor, though sometimes it is the faith of those praying for another rather than the faith of the one seeking healing. More importantly, faith at its heart is not believing God will do what we ask but trusting in Jesus Christ. Even if our specific request is not granted, we still trust in God, for God's love for us is not demonstrated fundamentally in answers to our prayers but in the cross of Jesus Christ.[16]

Seeing someone healed strengthens our faith almost as much as receiving healing ourselves. It is an occasion for rejoicing and giving thanks. But it is well to remember that not all healing is instantaneous; much occurs gradually over time in response to ongoing prayer. Yet as many will testify, simply participating in a healing service can deepen our relationship with God, even apart from whether we see our prayers answered at the time.

Our hope is in God. We do not always know how God will respond to the prayers of God's people. But we come to

God with expectant hope because we do know God's powerful life-giving Spirit is at work in the world, bringing healing, reconciliation, and love. We know as well a Savior who goes with us through all our times of suffering and grief as well as through our times of great joy. With Paul we are convinced that "neither death, nor life, nor angels, nor rulers, nor things present, nor things to come, nor powers, nor height, nor depth, nor anything else in all creation, will be able to separate us from the love of God in Christ Jesus our Lord" (Rom. 8:38-39).

Discussion Questions

1. What rhythms of worship have you experienced in your local church? What difference have they made in your life?

2. Have you ever participated in a Covenant Renewal Service or a reaffirmation of the Baptismal Covenant? How is making a new commitment to God helpful to our growth as Christians?

3. What does it mean to "remember your baptism"? How does the service itself assist in our experiencing anew all that God has done for our salvation, and how is this connected to what God does in baptism?

4. What would be the advantage of sharing our testimonies at a love feast? What difficulties do you see?

5. Have you ever participated in a healing service? If so, what did you hope for and what effect did it have on your faith? If not, what would encourage your participation and what would be an impediment?

Chapter 7

The Fifth Practice: Christian Community

TODAY MORE AND more people are seeking community. They have begun to question the cultural assumption that the essence of being human is to be a totally free, private individual and instead yearn for relationship. They are more suspicious of competition and more open to cooperation. They long for the sense of community that once marked city, town, and rural neighborhoods alike, and they are lonely in the midst of the huge numbers of people who crowd together in our cities and suburbs.

We are all made for relationship. Scripture does not depict either Israel or the church as a collection of individuals who decided to come together, but as the people of God, a community in which each person finds both relationship and identity. Community is essential to us as human beings and as Christians.

The desire for community today is most clearly seen in the small group movement. Sociologist Robert Wuthnow reports that "four out of every ten Americans belong to a small group that meets regularly and provides caring and support for its members."[1] That's an astonishing 75 million Americans. Moreover, two out of three of these groups are linked to churches or synagogues.[2] Within these groups the desire for relationship with one another is matched by a desire to experience God or enhance one's life spiritually.

Wuthnow's research shows these groups are having a profound impact on our society. "Not only are small groups attracting participants on an unprecedented scale," he says, "these groups are also affecting the ways in which we relate to each other and how we conceive of the sacred."[3] There are admirable strengths and worrisome weaknesses in the changes these small groups are bringing about.

The groups have indeed accomplished much. They have often provided strong community in which people "have found friends, received warm emotional support, and grown in their spirituality." Participants learn "how to forgive others and become more accepting of themselves." Some have overcome addictions. Many feel closer to God. Most "attend faithfully, usually at least once a week."[4] Small groups are providing a welcome alternative to the shallow relationships and impersonal institutions that mark American life.

Yet all is not well. For one thing, these small groups are very different from the extended families and close-knit communities of the past. You can choose your group, but you can't choose your family. While our responsibility to the group may involve a commitment of time and emotional energy, it is less than our obligation within a family. Groups enable easy bonding but also allow one just as easily to leave (an advantage in today's highly mobile society); families usually involve lifelong commitments.[5] When we recall that one image of the church is the "family of God," we might wonder if small groups as currently practiced can fulfill all that Christian community implies.

A second observation has to do with the nature of group interaction. Most small groups have an implicit rule that they are always to accept whatever anyone else in the group says. They place a high value on tolerance and emotional support, with the latter defined as "encouragement rather than criticism or guidance." "Caring for someone," notes Wuthnow, "is more likely to be defined . . . as not criticizing them rather than as trying to help them come to a different understanding."[6] The small group thus becomes a place to share one's thoughts and feelings without fear of being challenged. Given the way persons in the public arena regularly attack one another, the idea of the small group as a safe haven from criticism is attractive. But it comes at a heavy price: the loss of the kind of conversation that leads most readily to spiritual growth. The problem is that today it is hard to know how to speak forthrightly and lovingly at the same time.

A third concern by Wuthnow has to do with how we understand God. While most small group participants have a stronger sense of divine reality, "God is now less of an external authority and more of an internal presence."[7] "The deity of small groups," Wuthnow observes, "is a God of love, comfort, order, and security. Gone is the God of judgment, wrath, justice, mystery, and punishment."[8] Such a God, in Wuthnow's strong language, can become "domesticated," a divine "house pet that does our bidding," valued for help and encouragement but not evoking reverence or awe.[9] This is a God who never makes waves.

For those who grew up with a view of God as harsh, punitive, or distant, discovering a God who is loving, intimate, and personal can be revolutionary. From this perspective, what Wuthnow reports is a gain. But it too comes with a price: the loss of a full, rich knowledge of a God who also judges us out of love, is transcendent and mysterious (though not distant), and evokes reverence and awe as well as trust, hope, peace, and love.

Wuthnow additionally fears many small groups on the whole have jettisoned "the received wisdom embodied in formal creeds, doctrines, and ideologies," opting instead for "a pragmatic approach to solving one's problems," often through using prayer or Scripture as formulas for attaining the answers.[10] The focus of the group then shifts from God and the neighbor to address solely the needs of the participants. In this way, small groups may inhibit rather than encourage spiritual depth.

Wuthnow believes the small group movement "stands at an important crossroads in its history."[11] It can continue as it has, or it can challenge participants to a deeper spirituality. There is no question John Wesley would advise the latter course. More important, he has much to teach us on how to go about it, advice that addresses each of Wuthnow's concerns.

Discipline in Community

We saw earlier that to be a Methodist in Wesley's day was to commit yourself to a discipline. Called the "General Rules of the United Societies," this discipline provided early Methodists with a set of practices that aided their remaining in a relationship with God and their neighbor. Let me present in outline form the three rules of discipline:

> It is . . . expected of all who continue [in these Societies] that they should continue to evidence their desire of salvation,
> *First*, By doing no harm, by avoiding evil in every kind. . . .
> *Second*, By doing good, by being in every kind merciful after their power, as they have opportunity doing good of every possible sort . . . to all . . . : to their bodies . . . ;
> To their souls. . . .
> *Thirdly*, By attending upon all the ordinances of God. Such are:
> The public worship of God;
> The ministry of the word, either read or expounded;
> The Supper of the Lord;
> Family and private prayer;
> Searching the Scriptures; and
> Fasting, or abstinence.[12]

Wesley listed numerous specifics under rules one and two, some of which I will mention in a moment. But it is important first to get a sense of the three rules as a whole. The first involves refraining from actions we know to be irreverent to God or unloving to our neighbor. But it is not enough to refrain; we are called to act as well. The second rule includes those "works of mercy" that enact love for our neighbor, encompassing social concern ("bodies"), evangelism, and Christian formation ("souls"). The third rule includes those "works of piety" that enact our love for God; these strongly overlap the instituted means of grace.

To adopt this discipline as one's own was to leave behind one way of life in order to begin another. It was to turn away from such things as profaning the name of God, quarreling, engaging in uncharitable conversation, practicing dishonesty in business, and seeking to acquire needless wealth and possessions. It was to turn toward generosity to the poor, giving food to the hungry, visiting the sick and those in prison, instructing and exhorting others in the gospel, and living a life of worship and devotion to God.

To help Methodists keep this discipline, small groups were established. Originally the societies were the primary groups in the movement, but soon many became too large, with the societies in London and Bristol containing over one thousand members each. A plan to divide the Bristol society into classes of twelve in order to raise funds for a preaching chapel led Wesley to establish classes in all the societies, have them meet together once a week, and shift their purpose to accountability to the discipline.

The class became the doorway into Methodism. If one attended the weekly meetings and evidenced a desire to keep the discipline, then one would receive a ticket to the quarterly society meeting. Persistent failure to attend or to attempt to keep the discipline meant one would not receive

81

a ticket and would no longer be considered a member of the society.

David Lowes Watson highlights two central features of the weekly class meeting. First, there was a dialogue between the class leader and each member, the goal of which was accountability to the discipline. The purpose was not "to press for an intensive confessional, but rather a straightforward accounting of what had taken place during the preceding week."[13] That is, the central question was how the members had done that week in keeping to the discipline. The sharing of each person's stories made this "a process of mutual response and support," where participants learned from one another what it meant to be a disciple of Jesus Christ.

The second feature was the central role of the class leader. The leader was in effect pastor of the small group as well as spiritual guide. Ideal class leaders were individuals whose authority was due not to their position but to their love for group members and the insightful spiritual advice that they gave.

The role of the class meeting in maintaining accountability to the discipline can be seen more clearly when contrasted with the other central small group of Methodism, the band. Bands were smaller than classes, consisting of six to eight members, and they selected their own leaders. Their purpose was to assist those growing in sanctification by providing a place where members could "pour out their hearts without reserve, particularly with regard to the sin which did still 'easily beset' them, and the temptations which were most apt to prevail over them."[14]

In other words, the bands *were* an intense confessional, where matters embarrassingly difficult to discuss were brought before the group. The meetings were marked by mutual advice and prayer, often leading to close fellowship as members shared in each other's struggles. The focus of the bands on the sins and temptations of the heart is in sharp contrast to the class meetings with their emphasis on keeping the discipline. Joining a band was an option for any Methodist who had experienced justification and new birth; being a member of a class was a lifelong requirement of anyone who wanted to be a Methodist.

While the purpose of the class meeting was accountability, we would be wrong to conclude that fellowship was unimportant. It is possible to have close fellowship without adopting a discipline, but it is not possible to hold one another accountable to a discipline through regular meetings without fellowship developing. Wesley noted how class members "began to 'bear one another's burdens,' and 'naturally' to 'care for each other.' As they had daily a more intimate acquaintance with, so they had a more endeared affection for each other."[15] In this way, they "now happily experienced that Christian fellowship of which they had not so much as an idea before."[16]

Cell Groups Today

Many writers in the area of evangelism and church renewal are emphasizing the importance of small cell groups in the life of the church.[17] Some go so far as to predict that the only viable churches in the future will consist entirely of cell groups that meet weekly and then come together once a week for public worship.[18] We have certainly seen that in most of the notably growing churches around the world, their members participate in small groups.

The advantages of cell groups are many. They provide a way for people to become involved who would never set foot in a traditional church. They offer caring relationships, enabling people to experience "church" not as an institution or organization but as community. They encourage lay leadership and ministry.

The advice to have small groups does not in itself tell us what kind of group to have. There are many types of groups:[19] care and sharing, study, nurture, support, prayer, missional, evangelistic, and so on. Some churches see everything as a small group, including choir and church school classes. Often the groups have one primary purpose but incorporate other elements as well—prayer, for example, being an almost universal feature of group life. If there is a trend, it is away from informational to formational groups.

As we have seen, Wesley's small groups were for growth in the Christian life, and the classes assisted that growth through holding one another accountable to a discipline. The advantage of Wesley's approach is all the more evident when we recall Wuthnow's concerns. The discipline kept the Methodists focused on God and neighbor and on those practices that would help them know God more fully. The conversations within the group were focused on Christian growth. They sought and expected guidance as well as encouragement. Certainly they shared their life crises, discouragement, grief, and uncertainties, but these were discussed within the larger context of the Christian life. The resulting fellowship was, if anything, even deeper than that of many cell groups today.

Two of the best-known growing United Methodist churches use something like Wesley's class meetings. Ginghamsburg United Methodist Church in Tipp City, Ohio, has HOME (Homes Open for Ministry and Encouragement) groups that enable intimate relationship and reinforce the high expectations of the membership covenant.[20] Christ United Methodist Church in Fort Lauderdale, Florida, has Wesley Fellowship Groups that encourage "accountability in our walk with God."[21] Initially, each member of a Wesley Fellowship Group asks the group to hold him or her accountable for one thing, such as daily Scripture reading; later the group may agree to a common discipline.

Covenant discipleship groups are a contemporary appropriation of Wesley's class meetings. Developed by David Lowes Watson, they involve a group of eight to ten people who covenant with one another to follow a common discipline. Using Wesley's structure as a model, Watson proposes a four-fold discipline around acts of compassion and acts of justice (works of mercy) and acts of devotion and acts of worship (works of piety).[22] Each group then develops its own "covenant around these four rules, listing particular practices under each." The General Board of Discipleship publishes a number of resources to assist those who wish to form covenant discipleship groups.[23]

If we want to grow closer to God and increase in our love for others, there is no more effective means than accountability to a discipline and life together in a small group. Wesley combined the two in his class meetings. But whether we emulate his approach or find other ways to obtain the same end, we would be wise not to neglect these two important means of grace.

Christian Conference

We have noted the kinds of conversations that occurred in the classes and bands. They were ultimately aimed at helping Methodists to grow in love and in the process help them pray, worship, and serve more faithfully as well. Coming together to talk about such things is one aspect of Christian conference, itself a means of grace. Such conversations are all too rare in today's church.

There is another element of Christian conference that deserves our attention. Every year, John Wesley would meet with his brother Charles and other preachers to discuss matters of doctrine and discipline. It was at these annual conferences that Methodist teaching was clarified and direction was given to preaching and the nurture of the growing movement.

Today when many hear of a conversation about doctrine or theology, they assume it will involve using technical terms to deal with abstract concepts. While this may be intellectually stimulating, they think, at the end of the day doctrine just doesn't matter. It has little to do with the very practical concerns of life. After all, what really counts is not what is in your head but what is in your heart; what is important is not what you know but how you live.

This way of looking at doctrine would have puzzled John Wesley. Not that he wouldn't agree that being a Christian has to do with our heart and life, and simply assenting to doctrine with our minds falls far short of the new life that God offers us. He had no interest in "speculative" theology. But Wesley was vitally concerned with "practical divinity," which saw doctrine as important because it points us to God and teaches us how to live as faithful disciples. Our belief system is inextricably linked to how we pray and serve.

Wesley's understanding of doctrine as teaching that helps us practice our faith is rooted in a tradition that goes back to the New Testament. According to this tradition, what we believe about Christ or the church, for example, strongly determines our understanding of what salvation means or how we are to worship and serve God. Wesley's own conferences focused attention on the relation of grace and works and the nature of justification and sanctification, all vital to experiencing and living a Christian life.

Don Saliers and I have urged United Methodists to recover this Wesleyan practice of Christian conferencing and begin to talk together about what we believe and what difference it makes.[24] Just as the class meetings were occasions to discuss discipline, so there is also need for opportunities to discuss doctrine. Each local congregation could make such conversations a regular part of its life.

We can go about this any number of ways. For example, groups could discuss the Articles of Religion or the Confession of Faith found in *The United Methodist Book of Discipline*. They could also examine distinctive teachings of the Wesleyan tradition, using the *Discipline* or other helpful resources.[25] Or a group could discuss the affirmations found in the Apostles' or Nicene Creed.

The important thing is for the conversation to be not only about what we believe but also about what difference it makes. How does our doctrine point us to God? For what may we hope? How shall we live? What does it mean to be a faithful church? When our conversation about doctrine deals with questions like these, Christian conference becomes such a useful and important means of grace.

Of course, *how* we talk with one another is as important as what we talk about. Patient listening, respect for others, and avoiding name-calling and stereotypes are all necessary to practicing civil conversation. Saliers and I offer advice on this,[26] as did John Wesley some 250 years earlier.[27]

The central point is this: Our conversations should always be carried on in love. Our ability even to disagree in love is a witness to the gospel of Jesus Christ. It is not only the conclusions we reach about our beliefs that serve as means of grace but also the way we go about our discussions. As we seek to practice Christian conference in this way, the Holy Spirit enables us to grow in love for one another.

Discussion Questions

1. From your own experience, do you agree or disagree with Wuthnow's concern that small group conversation

encourages tolerance and affirmation at the expense of honest disagreement?

2. Do you agree or disagree with Wuthnow when he says we tend to "domesticate" God?

3. What are the advantages of our being held accountable to a discipline? Are there any dangers in doing this, and if so, how can we avoid them?

4. Are you currently or have you ever been a member of a small group? What kind of group was it? Did your participation help you grow as a Christian?

5. Many scholars say the first Christian affirmation of faith was to say "Jesus is Lord." What difference does it make in your life, your church, and the world for Jesus to be Lord?

6. Think of a controversial issue. If a group of Christians were to discuss that issue, what ground rules would be helpful in making the conversation both honest and loving?

Chapter 8

The Sixth Practice: Christian Lifestyle

SEVERAL YEARS AGO, I saw a book prominently displayed in an airport bookstore that offered seven steps to financial independence. Jesus told a rich young man how to have financial independence in only one step: "Go, sell your possessions, and give the money to the poor, and you will have treasure in heaven; then come, follow me" (Matt. 19:21). What we possess or desire can end up possessing us, determining our values, commitments, and lifestyle. Jesus' advice to this young man recognized what we so often miss—that how we live and what we value are directly related to our ability to be faithful disciples.

It was a point not missed by John Wesley. He warned the Methodists again and again of the danger of riches. Wesley was not simply protesting the way of life of the rich and famous. He saw the danger of riches to be as much in the desire to have or the endeavor to obtain them as in their actual possession. Moreover, he defined being rich as possessing "more of this world's goods" than is used according to the will of God.[1] He believed all that we have is a trust from God, to be used in the service of God's purposes.

To put it simply, Wesley believed we should only use for ourselves that portion of the world's goods that we need, and the rest we should give away. He was convinced we do not need as much as we think we do, and he was deeply committed to help those who had less than enough. The twentieth-century Methodist missionary E. Stanley Jones states this well: "Every person has a right to as much of the material things as will" enable him or her to be "mentally and spiritually and physically fit for the purposes of the kingdom of God. The rest belongs to the needs of others."[2]

Wesley's concern about the danger of riches was two-fold. He believed that even the desire for riches subtly but ever so certainly leads us to trust in them rather than God, making us unable to truly love God. Second, the desire to obtain or hold on to possessions impedes our ability to truly love our neighbor. In other words, riches can make the Christian life almost impossible.

These are strong claims. They are especially troubling when we remember that Wesley, following Scripture, defines being rich such that it includes most who are reading this book. We want to protest, saying, "No, it's not our having all these possessions; it's putting our trust in them. If the rich young man had not trusted in his wealth [which the passage doesn't actually say, though it is often inferred], then Jesus would not have told him to sell all his possessions and give the money to the poor." Then we breathe a sigh of relief and go on living exactly as we did before.

Yet before we think we have our lives nicely under control, we might ask ourselves *why* we want the possessions we have. What role do they play in our lives? After all, we are bombarded daily with commercials carefully designed by experts to make us desire more products. They appeal to a wide range of motives—status, success, sex appeal, beauty, even altruism—to get us to spend our money. Having things and the means to purchase them are how many give meaning to their lives. Our possessions and our income say much about who we are in society. The result is that our lives are marked by acquisition and consumption.

Living Simply

What is it that truly governs our lives? Are we actually as free to serve God and our neighbor as we would like to think we are? Let me suggest three practices that can help us decide whether and in what ways our possessions might be standing in the way of faithfulness to God.

First, we need opportunities to talk about our lifestyles. The early Methodists did this in their class and band meetings. They were able to help one another discern what faithful discipleship meant in terms of everyday life. Such conversations are all too rare in today's church. But for us to recover this practice would enable us to gain increasing clarity about how we should live as Christians in a world such as ours. It would be an invaluable means of putting God and our neighbor at the center of our lives.

Second, we need to resist the cultural pressures to give our lives meaning through consumption and possessions. Richard J. Foster calls this desire to have more "psychotic" because it has completely "lost touch with reality." He says, "We crave things we neither need nor enjoy. . . . We are made to feel ashamed to wear clothes or drive cars until they are worn out. The mass media have convinced us that to be out of step with fashion is to be out of step with reality."[3] How do we deal with such an unbalanced culture? One practical way suggested by Ronald J. Sider is simply to learn to laugh regularly at TV commercials. He proposes "developing family slogans like 'Who Are You Kidding?' and 'You Can't Take It with You!'" as responses to these calls to consume.[4] I have a friend who has a practice much like this, and his children now habitually make the same comments to the TV.

Third, we need to find ways to live more simply. Wesley's three rules for the use of money are a step in this direction. The first was *gain all you can* through honest labor, diligence, and wisdom, but never at the expense of our neighbor or (workaholics take note) in ways harmful to our health. The second, *save all you can,* was not a call to accumulate wealth but an admonition not to waste money by throwing it away on expensive or superfluous possessions or to gain the admiration of others. The third was the one even Wesley's Methodists found difficult, but Wesley believed was the key to everything: *Give all you can.* As stewards of all we have received, we are to use it all in ways that glorify God and manifest divine love.[5]

John Wesley lived faithfully according to these rules all of his adult life. Although his income continually increased, his lifestyle remained simple; he spent the same amount on himself each year and gave away more to relieve the poor. He had very few possessions, wore inexpensive clothes, and ate simple food.

In our century, lay evangelist Harry Denman in many ways emulated Wesley's lifestyle. He had no permanent residence and owned only one suit and coat. Though his work took him all over the world, he was famous for traveling with only a briefcase containing such necessary items as a change of underwear and a toothbrush. When congregations or admirers, distressed at the worn condition of his clothes, would give him a new suit or coat, he would give it away to someone who needed it worse than he did. Denman once said, "It is fun to see how little one can live on. Not having to keep up with the Joneses takes away much of the strain."[6]

Because Wesley and Denman were not driven by the desire to acquire, possess, consume, or advance, they were free to share gladly with others. In doing this, they saw themselves in small ways to be following Christ, who gave his life for all.

I confess I do not live as simply as Wesley or Denman. Perhaps you don't either. But we can make a start. We can begin to ask ourselves whether each potential purchase would really be pleasing to God. Suppose we identify one thing a month that we decide is really unnecessary to living a meaningful Christian life. Each time we make such a decision, we free ourselves that much more from the tyranny of things and for a life devoted to God.

Tithing

There are other ways we can begin to break the hold of money and possessions on our lives. One of these is tithing, that is, giving ten percent of our income to God. I do not present this as a divine command (although it has biblical warrant) but as a spiritual discipline. It is one way to structure our lives so that we do not forget that we belong to God and are citizens of God's kingdom. It is a form of gratitude to God for all our blessings, concretely expressed by directly returning to God a portion of our income.

Let me emphasize that we *need* to give in this way for the sake of our own spiritual health. It is one important way God uses to remake us into God's image. Tithing helps us stop thinking of money and possessions as "mine" and instead see them as God's.

To think that only ten percent of our income belongs to God is to misunderstand tithing. All that we own is received as a gift, entrusted to us by God to use for God's purposes. I once heard a story about a baptism in Appalachia, where a man was to be immersed in a river. A friend offered to hold his wallet while he got into the water. "No," he replied, "when the Lord gets me he gets my wallet, too."

This is why Wesley thought talk of "this or that proportion" being given to God was misleading. We should render to God "not a tenth, not a third, not half, but 'all that is God's,'" by employing our money on our own household, on the church, and on our neighbor in such a way that is faithful to God's word.[7] Ultimately it is not simply a percentage but our entire way of life that is at stake. How we handle our finances shows more than anything else what we truly believe is important.

In the spirit of Wesley, Ronald and Arbutus Sider decided to adopt a graduated tithe. They tried to calculate honestly their annual expenses, allowing "reasonable comfort but not all the luxuries." They then gave a tithe on their base figure and a graduated tithe beginning at fifteen percent on every thousand dollars above that. While they have had to refigure this over the years, it is a creative way to develop a lifestyle centered on generosity.[8]

You may be saying, "Wait a minute—I'd have trouble even making ten percent. This tithing idea is getting way out of hand." It is certainly the case that our circumstances can vary widely. Some of us may be at the poverty level or below and could use additional money just to meet basic needs. Some may face extraordinary medical expenses or unexpected home repair bills. Some of us are so in debt that we are having trouble just paying our monthly bills. Each person or family will have to decide for themselves what they can do. My plea is for searching honestly in examining our finances and finding a way to begin. Perhaps you can't give ten percent—what are you now giving? Can you increase it, for example, one percent a year? Through gradually increasing your giving, you will be surprised by how much you can do and by the kind of person you will become.

You may be wondering to what exactly you should give financially. As Wesley notes, the local church is one important recipient of giving. We give to the church not to maintain an institution but to further the mission of God. It is true that local churches do have expenditures for utility bills, insurance, and salaries as well as worship, curriculum, and outreach. But if the local church is not an end in itself but exists to worship and serve God and be the people of God, then these necessary expenses contribute to that goal.

We must also admit that the church is by no means perfect since it is we who make it up. Yet I would contend that any local church struggling to be faithful to God deserves our prayers and support.

In addition to the local church, there are many denominational and parachurch agencies that have enormously effective ministries and clearly further God's purposes in the world. United Methodists can be especially pleased with the United Methodist Committee on Relief (UMCOR), which is one of the finest and most efficient disaster-relief agencies in the world. It is only one example of the kind of organizations that merit our support.

Prayer and discernment are needed. How is God calling you to use your financial resources? While each person or family has to decide this individually, I would urge that this issue become part of our conversation in the Christian community. This is not so a group can tell anyone how they should give, but so together we can explore before God some possible ways to be faithful disciples in this area.

Fasting

Every time I drive to work, I see a billboard for a soft drink that urges us to "obey your thirst." This seems like common sense to us. Yet much of the Christian spiritual tradition would have found this worrisome. While we should certainly take care of our health, they would point out that obedience is due to God alone. Our desires can all too easily occupy the place in our lives that belongs to God.

Marjorie Thompson believes we live "as if there were no legitimate limits"; that is, we live in such a way that

> the appetites are given free reign. It is considered a God-given right to use every resource and creature on earth for personal enjoyment or gain. The goal of human life is to

acquire more, to experience more, to stimulate every sense to capacity and beyond. A life that recoginizes no limits cannot recognize the sovereignty of God.[9]

Food is something we desire and need. We are well aware that food is necessary to sustain our health but that too little or too much food (or too little of some kinds of food or too much of other kinds of food) can endanger health and life. What often does not occur to us is that it affects our spiritual life as well.

As Thompson observes, "Food is necessary to life, but we have made it more necessary than God." She asks, "How often have we neglected to remember God's presence when we would never consider neglecting to eat!"[10] In Wesley's language, this is a form of dissipation, in which something good and necessary to life begins to supplant God in our desires. What then seems a normal way of life to us is actually dangerously imbalanced.

Aware of the danger, Wesley advocated and practiced fasting as a way to reorder our lives. Fasting is the practice of intentionally abstaining from some or all food for a period of time. In his day as in ours, fasting was controversial. While "some exalted this beyond all Scripture and reason," said Wesley, "others utterly disregarded it," thereby "undervaluing as much as the former had overvalued it." For Wesley, "the truth lies between them both." Fasting "is not the end; but it is a precious means thereto."[11]

Wesley considered fasting one of the five instituted means of grace, that is, a practice directly ordained by God. It is found throughout Scripture. Jesus himself fasted and clearly assumed those who followed him would as well, beginning his teaching on the matter with the words "and whenever you fast" (Matt. 6:16). While fasting was not as popular among the early Methodists as the Lord's Supper or prayer, Wesley urged it continually and insisted his preachers practice it.

In his most extended discussion of fasting, Wesley made distinctions that remain helpful today. Like many before him, he warned against excessive fasting, "for we ought to preserve our health, as a good gift of God." We must take care, then, "to proportion the fast to our strength."[12] What counts as excessive will obviously vary from person to person, depending on his or her health and life circumstances. Richard Foster says, "Diabetics, expectant mothers, and heart patients should not fast."[13] Because it depletes our energy reserves, Marjorie Thompson advises against fasting during high-energy activities "such as travel, undue stress, or heavy physical labor."[14]

Wesley notes several degrees of fasting. While Scripture does describe fasting of forty days, much more typical are one-day fasts, from morning until evening. The early Christians not only practiced one-day fasts, they also had "half-fasts" on Wednesday and Friday, "on which they took no sustenance till three in the afternoon."[15] This was Wesley's own practice, observing both days from 1725 to 1738 and Friday only after 1738. As Steve Harper relates, Wesley would begin his fast "following the evening meal on Thursday" and would not eat again until Friday afternoon tea. He would take liquids such as "water, tea, or broth" if "necessary for his health."[16]

Another type of fasting is abstinence, which is "eating little; the abstaining in part; the taking of a smaller quantity of food than usual."[17] This is an especially attractive alternative for those whose health precludes a more total fast. In 1744, Wesley seems to be practicing a form of abstinence (and recommending his preachers do likewise) of eating only vegetables on Friday and toast and water in the mornings.[18]

The mildest form of fasting was "abstaining from pleasant food."[19] This form of fasting would be most useful to those with health problems or in occupations or situations that call for high expenditures of energy.

Whatever degree we choose, there are a number of ways fasting can enrich our spiritual lives. The most important is that it is an occasion to deepen our awareness of God. Countering the dissipating tendencies in our lives, it regularly returns our focus to God. "Fasting," says Dallas Willard, "confirms our utter dependence upon God by finding in him a source of sustenance beyond food."[20]

This is why we should not confuse fasting with dieting. Properly conducted, dieting has an admirable goal, namely bodily health. That can indeed be a welcome by-product of fasting. But the purpose of fasting is to re-center our lives upon God, enabling us to love and serve God more and to remain open to receive grace from God.

Because of this, fasting is often linked with prayer. Wesley notes that it is as fasting is used as a help to prayer "that it has so frequently been found a means, in the hand of God, of confirming and increasing . . . the love of God, and every holy and heavenly affection."[21] While we certainly practice prayer apart from fasting, it would be almost unnatural to practice fasting apart from prayer. Indeed, even as we go about our normal work, we may find ourselves continually thinking of and praying to God.

Because our thoughts are on God, we may also examine our lives before God, seeking guidance, forgiveness, and sanctifying grace. Wesley believed deep sorrow for sin was probably what originally led to the practice of fasting.[22] Persons today may well fast in times of sorrow or affliction. But even in ordinary times, fasting is an opportunity for the kind of self-examination before God that leads to growth as Christians.

One major benefit of fasting is, in Willard's words, that it "teaches temperance or self-control and therefore teaches moderation and restraint . . . to *all* our fundamental drives."[23] Willard echoes Wesley's observation about how we abuse good things by using them to excess.[24] Something as central to our lives as food will help moderate our other desires as well.

Marjorie Thompson takes this one step further, urging that we practice abstinence in all areas of our lives. For example, we could abstain from continual stimulation by the media, shopping sprees, even our heavy schedules and tendency to judge others or ourselves too harshly. The point is to abstain from or reduce whatever stands between us and God.[25]

A final benefit of fasting is that it helps set us free to serve God and our neighbor. "More than any other single Discipline," says Richard Foster, "fasting reveals the things that control us."[26] Those things are all the more dangerous because their control is so hidden. Fasting, by bringing them to light, can help restore in us the freedom to be who we were created to be, persons whose hearts and lives manifest God's love to the world.

Discussion Questions

1. Wesley warned Methodists strongly and repeatedly about the danger of riches. Do you believe his fears were well taken or exaggerated? How should Christians deal with possessions and money in our lives?

2. What ways can we resist cultural pressures (such as advertising) that encourage excess consumption?

3. Are Wesley's three rules for the use of money helpful today? If you were asked for guidelines on how Christians should use their money, what would you propose?

4. Why is tithing considered a spiritual discipline? How do tithing and other forms of disciplined giving help our growth as Christians?

5. Why do you think fasting is one of the spiritual disciplines likely to be practiced least? Do you see any benefit in fasting or in other forms of abstinence?

Chapter 9

The Seventh Practice: Serving Our Neighbor

ACCORDING TO Ronald J. Sider, "Most churches today are one-sided disasters." There are churches in the suburbs where "hundreds of people come to Jesus and praise God in brand-new buildings, but they seldom learn that their new faith has anything to do with wrenching, inner-city poverty just a few miles away." There are other churches where members "write their senators and lobby the mayor's office" but "would be stunned if someone asked them personally to invite their neighbors to accept Christ."[1]

It would be comforting to think that United Methodist churches do not fall into these one-sided categories, but I fear many do. Even more disturbing is that too many of our churches are neither sided; they have turned inward and neglect both evangelism and social concern. I'll say more about the problem of turning inward in the next chapter.

The one-sidedness that marks so many churches is in part an accident of American history. In the late nineteenth and early twentieth centuries, Christians began to divide into evangelistic and "social gospel" camps. Many advocates of evangelism saw a concern to improve social conditions as placing temporal problems ahead of eternal destiny; many adherents of the social gospel saw evangelism as promoting an individualistic, self-centered piety that distracted

Christians from caring for their neighbor. I still hear echoes of these criticisms in our churches today.

Of course, the matter is more complex than this, and there were many Christians who modeled a more holistic outreach.[2] One was E. Stanley Jones, who firmly believed "an individual gospel without a social gospel is a soul without a body and a social gospel without an individual gospel is a body without a soul. One is a ghost and the other a corpse."[3]

Although writing this in the 1970s, Jones was the spiritual descendant of an earlier nineteenth-century tradition in which those most associated with evangelism, revivals, and camp meetings were at the same time the most likely to be in the forefront of movements to abolish slavery, give equal rights to women, and combat poverty.[4] It was no accident that many of these were Wesleyans, for they saw a commitment to love their neighbor through evangelism and social reform as the necessary consequence of the sanctified life.

For Wesley, practices of evangelism and social concern were both manifestations of a life governed by love and an explicit element of Methodist discipline. The first rule of discipline ("doing no harm") was intended to help Methodists refrain from those actions that harmed others as well as themselves. The second rule urged them to

> evidence their desire of salvation by doing good of every possible sort, and as far as possible, to all . . . :
> To their bodies . . . by giving food to the hungry, by clothing the naked, by visiting and helping them that are sick, or in prison.
> To their souls by instructing, reproving, or exhorting.[5]

These "works of mercy" through which we reach out in love to our neighbor are every bit as vital to our growth as Christians as "works of piety" such as prayer, searching the Scripture, and the Lord's Supper. It is through these practices that we directly participate in God's great mission to renew the earth in love.

In this chapter, our focus will be on those practices related to social concern. In doing this, we are part of a tradition that stretches from our current Social Principles[6] back to John Wesley himself. More important, it reflects the conviction that concern for the poor, for working people, racial and gender equality, the environment, and the like must be central to our faith because they matter deeply to God.

Loving Our Neighbor

We are created to love. We are meant to give of ourselves to others. E. Stanley Jones believed it is encoded in our very being. "The most miserable people in the world," he said, "are the people who are self-centered, who won't do anything for anybody, except themselves." In contrast, "the happiest people are the people who deliberately take on themselves the sorrows and troubles of others. Their hearts sing with a strange wild joy."[7] There is no richer or more fulfilling life than one in which love is put into action.

Many Christians have enacted love through participation in ongoing outreach ministries. While I was a pastor in Atlanta, God gave a member of a nearby Baptist church a vision for a food pantry that could serve the poor of our neighborhood. His enthusiasm and commitment led several churches, including my own, to partner in establishing and staffing this ministry. It was certainly important to those needing assistance, but it was also important for the churches and individuals who maintained it, for it enabled them to grow in love through serving others.

Other Christians regularly volunteer at homeless shelters, and many churches help staff "soup kitchens" that provide a free hot meal for those on the street. One church I know not only provides the meal but decorates the tables their guests use. Then they provide refills of tea and coffee, engage in conversation, and do anything else they can think of to make their guests welcome.

Short-term mission events have become more prominent in the lives of many local churches. These usually involve travel to another city, state, or country for one or two weeks. Volunteers in Mission provides opportunities to participate in a wide range of mission projects. As I write this, one church I know has a VIM team in Mexico erecting buildings at a church camp and teaching vacation Bible school. Other projects could include offering medical assistance in Haiti, constructing a church in Jamaica, or drilling wells in Mozambique.

Habitat for Humanity is another sponsor of short-term mission projects, using volunteers to build inexpensive homes for persons on low incomes. The Appalachian Service Project provides opportunities to serve in one of the poorest areas of the United States. There are many more such agencies as well as events planned and sponsored by local churches.

Sometimes a short-term project can become a long-term commitment. Michael Slaughter, pastor of Ginghamsburg UMC, tells of their "Adopt a Christmas Family" program in 1979. Their study of biblical teaching on the poor led to an agreement "to spend on a family in need the same amount we would spend on our family." Slaughter said,

> The leading of the Spirit was clear. If you bought your child a new bike, you would buy another child a new bike. Why was a used bike good enough for someone else's child, if it wasn't good enough for your own? If you bought your child name-brand clothes, then you would buy another child name-brand clothes.[8]

The church members met their "adopted" families, purchased their gifts, and had a joyous celebration at a

Christmas Eve Candlelight Service. But they sensed God calling them to love more deeply. To really love as Christ loved, they would need to be involved with these families not just one day but every day of the year.

This meant financial commitment: "When I buy my kids' back-to-school clothes, I will buy my Christmas family back-to-school clothes, too." But it also meant developing a relationship with families over time, giving them their phone numbers and getting to know them as persons. Slaughter sees this as a vital cause of spiritual renewal in his church.[9]

Whether through long-term relationships like this or through shorter-term encounters like a VIM trip or Habitat project, our truly coming to know the people we serve is vital to our spiritual growth. One reason is that it helps us get rid of harmful stereotypes and misinformation that keep us from being all that God intends. Wesley's words on this are as applicable to our day as they were in his:

> One great reason why the rich in general have so little sympathy for the poor is because they so seldom visit them. Hence it is that . . . one part of the world does not know what the other suffers. Many of them do not know, because they do not care to know: they keep out of the way of knowing it—and then plead their voluntary ignorance as an excuse for their hardness of heart.[10]

A second reason is that we will find ourselves enriched by relationships with persons whose life circumstances are so different from our own. We certainly can learn from them a greater appreciation for how much we now take for granted. But there are deeper lessons. We may meet people who model extraordinary generosity or hospitality, graciously sharing out of limited resources. We may find persons whose focus is not on competing to get ahead but on helping one another to make it through life. We may encounter people suffering great adversity but demonstrating deep and abiding faith in the midst of it all.

That was what happened to Dick Wills. Weary from years of trying to be a successful pastor, he sought to get away. On the advice of a friend, he applied and was accepted to attend a regional seminar of the World Methodist Evangelism Institute. He thought he was applying for the meeting in Tahiti, but that was a year away—he was accepted for the conference in South Africa.

It changed his life.

Most of the people who attended were from central and southern Africa. They "were very poor and enduring great hardships." Wills relates that

> I was immediately struck by their obvious joy. I began to wonder how these people, living under such difficult and violent conditions could have such joy? It was a stark contrast to my own situation. I live in one of the most affluent areas of Fort Lauderdale, Florida. . . . I had every mark of success. Why was it these people in Africa had this joy and I did not?[11]

Wills experienced a rebirth and learned an important truth: "Joy comes from walking with God and is not dependent on external circumstances."[12] Even though Wills would not claim that his participation in this conference was motivated by care for others, the Holy Spirit used the encounter with African Christians as a means of grace to impart new life. Sometimes if we simply follow God's leading, even without the motivation, we will find God will use what we do to change our hearts.

Care for the Earth

In my ninth-grade biology class in 1963, I read Rachel Carson's newly published *Silent Spring*. This warning that we were dangerously polluting our environment is generally considered to be the beginning of the environmental movement. At the time, I was not a Christian and did not connect ecological concern with discipleship. However, I suspect that my Christian classmates did not make that connection either. Christianity, especially in its Roman Catholic and Protestant varieties, had focused strongly on human salvation while allowing scriptural teaching on the creation to slip into the background.

There were exceptions to this. Eastern Orthodoxy has on the whole done a better job of preserving an emphasis on God's love for creation than have Christians in the West. St. Francis of Assisi is perhaps the most prominent Western Christian to emphasize care for all of creation. Then there is John Wesley, who taught love for God's creation and most especially for animals, who so often suffer at human hands.

Wesley believed God was a wise creator and governor, who loves all creation. Humanity was "God's viceregent upon earth," the "channel of conveyance" through which "all the blessings of God flowed" to the creation.[13] Through falling into sin, humanity became "incapable of transmitting those blessings," necessarily cutting off the communication between the Creator and creation.[14] The result is that the creation itself suffers at the hands of humanity, who, instead of conveying God's blessings, uses creation for its own ends, selfishly and unwisely. If sanctification is about restoring the image of God in us, then Christian growth necessarily involves our reflecting the same care God has for creation.

Today we are far more aware than Wesley of the damage we have done to our environment. The pollution of the air and water, overconsumption of finite resources, wasteful lifestyles, massive deforestation, elimination of habitats and extinction of species, and depletion of the ozone layer are all well known to the general public as well as science. The problems are real and often urgent.

As important as these concerns are, it might seem odd that they are placed in a chapter on serving our neighbor. Yet all of us call this planet home, and all of us have a stake in having a safe, healthy environment and in conserving resources so that our global neighbors as well as future generations will have enough. We receive this world as a gift from God, that we might not only use it responsibly but also enjoy its many wonders and great beauty.

Many Christians and local churches have undertaken environmental ministries along with the more traditional activities designed to help persons directly. Recycling is one practical way we can avoid waste and preserve resources. Some churches have even become recycling centers where neighborhood residents can bring used paper, cans, and bottles.

Tony Campolo suggests churches organize a "Releaf" campaign to plant trees in urban areas. He notes that trees are one of the best antidotes to excess carbon dioxide in the atmosphere. Their shade saves on air conditioning costs, and they help lower heating bills by protecting against winter winds. They also reintroduce the natural environment into our cities.[15] We can also use recycled paper and purchase church supplies from environmentally aware companies. Local churches can be insulated to lessen energy use.[16] As individuals, we can seek ways to conserve water and energy. We can avoid purchasing products in aerosol cans. In the spirit of Wesley, we can find ways to care especially for the animals with whom we share our planet.

These are as much a part of Christian discipleship as feeding the hungry or visiting the sick. As we practice care for the creation, we not only make our world safer for generations to come but begin to acquire some of the loving characteristics of God. Our lives are not only enriched by a cleaner environment and the conservation of nature but also by becoming once again faithful stewards over this world God has given us.

The Big Picture

Problems such as world hunger, human rights abuse, environmental destruction, drug and alcohol addiction, racial and ethnic conflict, sex and violence in the media, poverty, and disease can seem overwhelming. Even if we engage in practices as individuals, families, and local churches that truly manifest God's love, they may seem insignificant from this larger perspective. Yet they are of great importance. These practices not only are vehicles of the transforming reality of God's love, but they also nurture real hope in a world that is all too often marked by suffering, pain, and injustice. Furthermore, Christians can practice a more holistic caring combining deeds with sharing our faith in a way that government cannot.

Still, there is a role for Christian involvement in the political arena itself. Many of these problems are national and global in scope, involving powerful economic and social forces. Only government action or the protest of large numbers of well-organized citizens can effect change on this level.

We should acknowledge immediately that there are many thoughtful Christians who would dissent from some of what I have just said. They believe there is great danger in Christian involvement in politics because by its very nature politics is a means of gaining and exercising power. Even if the intentions are good, they would say, politics and government entail a very different kind of power from the power of the cross. For them, the task of the church is not to change society but to model an alternative to the prevailing values of society.

There is much to commend in this criticism. It certainly is the primary task of the church to order its life according to the kingdom of God. There is also wisdom in warning of the dangers of seeking political power, not the least of which is the temptation to let the ends justify the means. Even so, there are many examples of Christians who faithfully used political involvement to work for social justice.

One was William Wilberforce, a member of the British Parliament and contemporary of John Wesley. Motivated by his deep faith in Christ, Wilberforce led the fight that ended the slave trade and eventually abolished slavery altogether in Great Britain. The last letter written by Wesley, only a week before his death, was to Wilberforce, encouraging him in his efforts to end slavery.

Wesley and Wilberforce were convinced that slavery was contrary to God's reign and a violation of God's love. They took seriously the biblical claim that the God worshiped by Israel was the ruler of the nations and that the risen Jesus was Lord of all. As a result, they were able to discern great evil in a practice that most in their day took for granted.

The problem with sin that is embedded in culture itself is that it seems so normal. When I grew up in the South in the 1950s, racial segregation was seen as natural by most whites, simply a part of everyday life. It had its own social justification, to which most churches readily acquiesced, gave biblical sanction, and embodied in their own congregational life. Thanks to courageous advocates for change, we see now how evil racism and segregation are, and many Christians no longer falsely interpret Scripture through that cultural lens.

As Ronald Sider notes, one reason some contemporary Christians miss seeing social evil is that they "see sin almost exclusively in personal terms," as "things like lying, stealing, drunkenness, and adultery." These "are wrong, terribly wrong. But so are racism and economic oppression."[17]

So how do we come to see our world more as God sees it? And, how shall we go about working for social change?

We can begin by searching the Scriptures to see what God teaches us concerning social and economic issues. In doing so, we must remember that this involves prayerful and informed interpretation. Some matters, such as God's concern for the poor and the victims of injustice, will be obvious and pervasive. Other issues will require a consideration of the historical and cultural context in conjunction with the overall teaching of Scripture. Many Christians, for example, believe the scriptural passages that refer to slavery do not imply acceptance but lay the foundations for its abolition; the same could be said about issues of gender inequality. Also, we should not expect Scripture to speak precisely on many contemporary issues but rather to provide us with a perspective that will enable us to analyze and address them.

We will also need to study the issues themselves, drawing on contemporary research and analysis. Because these issues are controversial, we may need to examine a range of alternative views to be fully informed. We should also study carefully the Social Principles of The United Methodist Church, which is the official teaching of our denomination on social issues.

The early Christians, living at the time of the Roman Empire, had very limited influence on political decisions. Today Christians in America are citizens in a democracy and have a wide range of options unknown to the New Testament church. We can write our elected representatives on behalf of legislation, complain to company executives about unfair practices, and send letters to ambassadors and governmental leaders protesting human rights abuses. We can join with other citizens to support causes we believe are biblically just. We can campaign for and vote to elect those candidates that best support our values and vision.

We must remember as we engage in these practices that Christians will not agree on all issues. We do not always interpret Scripture the same way, nor do we all share the same understanding of society or politics. Scripture does not prescribe one political system as normative, and this means we will have to make judgments about such things as the proper role of government in the economic system. Put differently, while Christians are clearly called to alleviate suffering, bring justice to the oppressed, strengthen families, feed the hungry, and care for the earth, they may disagree on how best to attain these goals as well as which are most important at this time. What we all should avoid is being captured by any single political ideology or party, for our allegiance is to the kingdom of God. As Tony Campolo says, Jesus is neither a Republican nor a Democrat.[18]

I read recently of a secular camp for boys and girls that forbids any overt expression of religion by those attending. A counselor said that participants must leave their religion at the door. While the question about what religious practices should be permitted in such a diverse setting is valid, the counselor's comment is not. Any faith that one can leave at the door is not worth having. Being Christian is not simply having a private set of beliefs and practices. It is who we are at the core of our identity. Our Christian life goes wherever we go—and that includes the hearing at city hall, the voting booth, and the shopping mall. We are called to be always and everywhere God's people and to participate in God's mission of love and justice in the world.

Discussion Questions

1. Is Ronald Sider's observation that "most churches . . . are one-sided disasters" true to your experience? Do you

know of local churches that are not? How can churches embrace more faithfully the fullness of God's mission?

2. Have you participated in either a short-term mission project or ongoing outreach ministry of your local church? Or have you found other ways to be in ministry to your neighbor? How effective was this project or ministry in meeting human needs? What impact did participation in it have on your own growth as a Christian?

3. Discuss ways your church or family can contribute to caring for creation.

4. Do you believe Christians should be involved in politics? How would you go about forming a Christian perspective on an issue? What ways would you choose to work for social change?

5. Obtain a copy of the Social Principles of The United Methodist Church (it can be found in *The Book of Discipline*). Do you believe these are a faithful reflection of Scripture and the reign of God as you understand them?

Chapter 10

The Eighth Practice: Sharing Our Faith

WITH THE CRUCIFIXION of Jesus, all the hopes of his disciples collapsed. They may not have fully understood him, but they trusted him and became his followers. Like the two disheartened disciples on the Emmaus road, they "had hoped that he was the one to redeem Israel" (Luke 24:21). But death had a finality to it. The story was over. The world wasn't going to change. It was now time to move on.

It was in the midst of this despair that the resurrection of Jesus from the dead exploded into human history.

Jesus' resurrection was unparalleled as an event and revolutionary in its consequences. Sin and death had been overcome. A new creation had begun. One of the cruelest instruments of death ever devised had now become the greatest expression of God's love and the means to new life. Jesus was alive, never to die again, with us "always, to the end of the age" (Matt. 28:20).

When he began his ministry, Jesus had announced, "The time is fulfilled, and the kingdom of God has come near; repent, and believe in the good news" (Mark 1:15). He both proclaimed and demonstrated the power of the Kingdom. He taught people to forgive others as they have been forgiven, that whoever would be greatest should serve others, what it means to love one's neighbor, and one's need to trust in God.

He ate with sinners, conversed with women, spent time with children, and even touched people with leprosy. He healed the sick, cast out demons, stilled storms, and brought the dead back to life.

This was amazingly good news to many but not to all. Jesus' ministry challenged conventional assumptions about social status, religious piety, proper behavior, and the nature of power. His death would simply confirm that his message was mistaken and his way of life a failure. But death is not the end of the story. Jesus is alive, raised from the dead. The last word does not belong to death but to life—not to sin but to love. The life that is eternal is centered not on acquiring possessions, power, or status but on serving God and our neighbor. There really is hope for those who suffer, dignity for those looked down upon, forgiveness and new life for sinners, and a peace that can never be taken away.

Having received this life-transforming message, early Christians, empowered by the Holy Spirit, began to share the good news throughout the Mediterranean world. Such sharing is called evangelism, a term derived from the New Testament word *euangelion*, meaning "good message." At the heart of the message was what God had done in Jesus Christ. As Mortimer Arias has said, "Jesus Christ is both the evangel and the evangelizer. . . . He is the center and content of the gospel, and he is the first evangelist of the kingdom."[1] Because the crucified Jesus was risen, his life was seen to embody the kingdom of God itself—God's will lived out in this world of sin, suffering, and death. By proclaiming *this,* Jesus as Savior and Lord, is it any wonder the early Christians were accused of "turning the world upside down" (Acts 17:6)?

The tragic reality is that the world already is upside down; it is God's mission to set it right again. In Jesus Christ, God has begun to do just that. Our announcement of this divine victory over sin and death is God's primary means of renewing our world.

Thus the commission Jesus gives to the disciples at the end of Matthew is ours as well: "All authority in heaven and on earth has been given to me. Go therefore and make disciples of all nations" (Matt.28:18-19). We are likewise recipients of Jesus' promise in Acts: "But you will receive power when the Holy Spirit has come upon you; and you will be my witnesses in Jerusalem, in all Judea and Samaria, and to the ends of the earth" (Acts 1:8).

We might wonder why God has chosen to operate in this way. Why not, for example, simply reach everyone directly, or for that matter raise multiple chosen nations alongside Israel? Depending on us to share this good news seems inefficient, perhaps even risky.

I think the clue is in phrases like "all nations" and "to the ends of the earth." God could of course deal directly with each individual, making evangelism unnecessary, or with every nationality or ethnic group, restricting our evangelism to people just like us. But God's mission is not only to restore our relationship with God but also to rebuild loving relationships among people.

God desires neither to leave us all divided from one another, whether as individuals or nations, nor to have us lose our distinctive personalities or cultures. Instead, God wants to knit us together in love while retaining the richness of our diverse personalities and cultural heritages. The ultimate goal is the restored humanity described by John of Patmos, who in his vision saw "a great multitude that no one could count, from every nation, from all tribes and peoples and languages," standing together as one to give praise to God for their salvation (Rev. 7:9-10).

Sharing the Good News

If the news is this good, why do most of us not share it more readily? As Eddie Fox and George Morris observe, many find it "easier to do the deed of the gospel than to name the name of Jesus Christ."[2] When I ask this question in seminary classes or local church workshops, a number of reasons are given.

First, some have had bad experiences from so-called evangelism—condemnatory preaching, pushy strangers wanting to know if we've been saved, people showing up at our doorstep, acquaintances prepared to argue at length to get us to adopt their beliefs. In fairness, we should acknowledge that some of these folks mean well. But fearing we will be seen in the same way as they are, we refrain from evangelism.

Related to this is a change in American culture. Religion is increasingly seen as a private matter, something we keep to ourselves. We are afraid sharing our faith with others will be seen as a violation of cultural propriety.

Some think that evangelism is a good thing but that they do not know enough to do it. Evangelism, they believe, is the task of experts, not ordinary Christians like themselves.

Fox and Morris believe we are reluctant to share our faith because it is risky. "A human is never more vulnerable," they note, "than when he or she raises to the level of speech the deepest thoughts, commitments, and desires of life."[3] To offer another that which is most precious to us is to risk rejection.

Given these reasons, Rebecca Manley Pippert is right to say that what keeps us from evangelism is not ignorance but fear: "We fear that our friends will reject or marginalize us if we speak about our faith; we fear that what we don't know will be exposed; we fear that our beliefs will be challenged."[4] The best way we can address these fears is to gain confidence in our ability to share our faith in ways that are genuine and non-manipulative.

We can begin by being clear about our motive. It is neither to add more members to keep our church alive nor to gain recognition for our evangelistic achievements. The only authentic motive, besides obedience to Christ's command, is *love* for others. We have received a wonderful gift of new life, and we want to let others know they can receive this gift as well.

Second, this faith-sharing occurs in *relationships*. We do not accost strangers on the street but share our faith with people we know—friends, co-workers, and family. The reason for this is simple: Effective faith-sharing requires "mutual trust and respect,"[5] and that is found most readily in existing social networks. In any relationship involving mutual sharing, it is both natural and appropriate for a Christian from time to time to describe the difference Christ is making in his or her life. The model for this sharing, as Fox and Morris note, is not a monologue (teacher to student or salesperson to customer) but a dialogue between friends.[6]

Because faith-sharing is a dialogue, it involves *listening* as much as or more than it does speaking. Many people are desperate for someone who will listen to them with genuine compassion and understanding. Such listening is a ministry in itself, but it also can open the door to conversation about Christ. Listening is often harder for us than speaking, but with patience and practice it can be learned.[7]

Fortunately, when we do speak, we do not have to have all the answers. We can be *honest* about our struggles and shortcomings. Such honesty, says Pippert, "shatters the stereotype that all Christians are judgmental and critical people."[8] As Harry Denman pointed out, being vulnerable in this way puts us on the same ground with everyone else and relieves us from having "to be an expert in order to witness."[9]

What we do share is *our own story*, the difference Jesus Christ has made in our lives. The absolutely critical point of faith-sharing, in the words of Fox and Morris, is this: "We do not tell people why they should believe or what they should believe. We tell them why and what we believe."[10] In other words, our task is not to try to argue people into the faith. People are naturally resistant to someone else telling them what to do or believe, but they are usually interested in hearing what has "worked" in someone's life. Sharing something of your own experience with God, whether in a time of crisis or as part of everyday life, will often lead a friend or co-worker to want to know more.

I should note that while existing social networks are the most natural avenues for faith-sharing, there is still a need to share our faith with strangers. Christians so often do not frequent the places where non-Christians gather or have them as friends. Fox and Morris have sound advice on how to practice this form of evangelism.[11] Certainly the need for sensitive listening is even greater with strangers, for in the encounter is the potential for a new relationship.

For many, the most difficult aspect of faith-sharing is *inviting* another person to receive Christ as his or her Savior and Lord. There is no one way to do this. It requires our sensitivity to the receptivity of the other person as well as the leading of the Holy Spirit. Often we will find persons who want to receive Christ but don't know how. Again, Fox and Morris have helpful advice, including a sample prayer for a new Christian.[12]

Faith-sharing removes a heavy burden when it reminds us that we do not convert anyone—conversion is the work of the Holy Spirit. What we do is simply share our faith. Should someone not be interested or decline our invitation to receive Christ, we must respect that decision and continue to love the person. We need not lose hope but must not try to force a positive response. The integrity of his or her response depends on its being freely given, and the integrity of our evangelism depends on non-manipulative, caring love.

How, then, can we learn to share our faith with others? We can begin by sharing it with one another. One reason the early Methodists shared their faith so naturally was that it was an integral part of their weekly class and band meetings and quarterly love feasts. They knew how to speak of Christ in their everyday lives to others because they regularly did so together. For us to find opportunities to do so today would be the greatest single thing we can do to learn faith-sharing.

Second, we can study together some of the excellent resources that are now available to develop our faith-sharing skills.[13]

Third, we can begin to list persons we know who may not have heard the good news. We can then include their names in our prayers to God, asking that we be given opportunities to share with them what Christ means in our lives and that they come to know God's love in Christ in their own.

Welcoming the Stranger

I am sometimes invited to teach in church school classes. Not wanting to run the risk of being late, I often arrive early. More often than not, what I find when I enter the classroom are people happily conversing and busily consuming coffee and donuts. I have stood watching this fellowship for as long as ten minutes, until someone finally notices me or the program chair arrives.

These classes without fail describe themselves as friendly. It is a fair description—I saw it with my own eyes! However, they were not initially friendly with me, a stranger in their midst. They did not know how to welcome someone not already a member of their group.

Turning inward in this way is only natural for church school classes and local churches. In part, it has to do with enjoying one another's company; it also is due to all having a stake in preserving an institution that has great meaning for their lives. The result is a bias against change and sometimes the erection of hidden barriers for new persons who want to be a part of the fellowship.

How do strangers experience your congregation? Much practical advice is available today to assist churches in becoming more welcoming.[14] Beyond the obvious matter of having genuinely friendly greeters and ushers, this includes having a clean, well-kept building, signs to direct newcomers to classrooms and restrooms, and a bright, clean, well-tended nursery.

There are two ways we can increase our sensitivity to how our church is experienced by newcomers. First, we can interview our newest members (or, if possible, visitors who chose not to return) to discover their first impressions of our church. Second, we can become strangers ourselves and visit other churches. While our experience will not mirror that of those persons of little or no Christian background who increasingly populate our communities, it will tell us much about how it feels to be in a new and unfamiliar setting.

But as important as these concerns are, welcoming the stranger has a more profound meaning. It is one aspect of the practice of hospitality,[15] which has deeply biblical roots. We see examples of this in the hospitality Abraham and Sarah offered to three strangers (Gen. 18) and in Paul's urging the church in Rome to "extend hospitality to strangers" (Rom. 12:13).

Hospitality is not the work of a committee "but a congregational lifestyle,"[16] a way of being as much as a way of doing. As Roger Swanson and Shirley Clement say so well, "There is no more effective witness to the universal offer of God's grace through Jesus Christ than a congregation offering a genuine welcome to persons whomever and wherever they are."[17] The key is really caring for people outside as well as inside the congregation.

What draws seekers to our churches? Often it is an invitation by someone in the church. In fact, survey after survey has shown the number one reason people begin attending a church is that someone invited them. The most effective invitations are specific: not "I hope you'll visit our church someday" but "why don't you come next Sunday?" Special services, worship services in a particular style, church school classes, or small group meetings often provide good reasons to extend an invitation. Since coming to a new place is an uncomfortable experience for some, the offer to bring or meet them there can help put a first-time visitor at ease.

People are also drawn by a church's reputation and the witness of the lives of its members. Pippert notes, "When we live as Jesus did, in his power and with his presence, seekers will be drawn to us."[18] As Swanson and Clement observe, "Congregations that are welcoming, flexible, genuine, and patient in love will not lack for seekers after God at their doors and in their pews."[19]

Entering New Life

Hospitality involves more than greeting newcomers warmly and making them feel at home. People have a need to become involved in the life of the church. Swanson and Clement believe many churches "make a serious error in leaving new members alone." Studies show that the primary reason up to half of new members in mainline congregations become inactive after one year is that they were not given the opportunity to serve.[20]

Inclusion into the life of the church can be a means of evangelizing seekers as much as involving new members. George G. Hunter III tells of how he became a Christian through becoming involved in youth activities and worship at Fulford Methodist Church. He was given a warm welcome, was fully included in the fellowship, had many conversations about the gospel, and was encouraged by the pastor and others. Hunter "observed people seriously, and adventurously, living their lives as credible Christians." It was, he relates, "within, say, three months I found myself believing what these people believed" and soon "prayed a prayer inviting the Spirit of Christ into my life 'as Savior and Lord.'"[21] It was through participation in the church with Christians that Hunter himself became a Christian.

None of this would surprise John Wesley. Those who were "awakened" to their sins (the seekers of his day) began attending class and society meetings as well as the parish church. In the Methodist meetings, they were able to meet, converse, and join in ministry with Christians. While their coming to justifying faith was a work of the Spirit, the class and society meetings were a prime environment for the Spirit's work.

William Abraham takes this a step further by defining evangelism as "initiation into the kingdom of God."[22] Abraham worries that to define evangelism as simply proclamation or church growth is insufficient, for it can leave us with persons who have made a decision for Christ or joined the church but not really entered into the Christian life. To remedy this, he proposes six practices into which everyone should be initiated before evangelism is complete. These he names as conversion, baptism, the "rule of life" (beginning to learn how to love God and our neighbor), the rule of faith (learning the basic teachings of Christianity by way of a historic creed), life in the Spirit (discovering which gifts of the Spirit for ministry one has been given), and spiritual disciplines (beginning to practice means of grace such as the Eucharist, prayer, and devotional reading of Scripture).[23]

There are a number of ways to make something like this a normal expectation for persons coming into the Christian faith. One is the recovery of the ancient church practice of enrolling interested seekers into a catechumenate. The catechumens (meaning "hearers") would attend the preaching and prayers of corporate worship and also regularly meet together with a leader to learn how to live a life of prayer and service. Those desiring to become Christians went through an intensive time of prayer and fasting during Lent, were baptized at the Easter vigil, and then received communion for the first time. Afterward, they were given instruction in the basic teachings of the faith. Daniel T. Benedict has proposed a contemporary version of this practice for United Methodists.[24]

Another approach is that of Ginghamsburg United Methodist Church and other churches that have high expectations for new members. Persons at Ginghamsburg who seek to become members are enrolled in a three-month course called Vital Christianity. Attendance is mandatory; "missed classes must be made up." At the end of the class, each person then decides if he or she will undertake the responsibilities of covenant membership, including "active stewardship, worship attendance, participation in a service-outreach ministry, and involvement in a small group."[25] Some "High Expectation" churches have a series of courses, each leading to deeper commitment and greater growth.

While these various approaches are not identical, they all witness to a single truth: Being a Christian is at its heart a hunger for God and a compassion for one's neighbor. God seeks to renew our hearts in love and to make us once again the people we were created to be. God does so as we engage in life-enriching practices. It is a tragedy to settle for anything less. It is our greatest joy to receive life from God in all its fullness.

As you therefore have received Christ Jesus the Lord, continue to live your lives in him, rooted and built up in him and established in the faith, just as you were taught, abounding in thanksgiving. (Col. 2:6)

125

Discussion Questions

1. If you were asked what is so good about the good news, what would you say?

2. Why do you think many Christians have difficulty sharing their faith? Do you find faith-sharing difficult? Why or why not?

3. What difference has faith in Jesus Christ made in your life?

4. What are some ways your congregation or church school class can make visitors feel more welcome? What can you do to extend hospitality to visitors?

5. How can your church help new members and seekers enter into a relationship with Jesus Christ?

Notes

Notes to Chapter 1

1. Richard J. Foster, *Celebration of Discipline: The Path to Spiritual Growth* (San Francisco: Harper & Row, 1978), 2.
2. For a more detailed discussion see Henry H. Knight III, *The Presence of God in the Christian Life: John Wesley and the Means of Grace* (Metuchen, N.J.: Scarecrow Press, 1992), 8-15.
3. John Wesley, "An Earnest Appeal to Men of Reason and Religion," *Works* 11:46.
4. Hymn 287, *The United Methodist Hymnal* (Nashville: The United Methodist Publishing House, 1989).
5. Luke Timothy Johnson, *Living Jesus: Learning the Heart of the Gospel* (San Francisco: HarperCollins, 1999), 4-5.
6. Cornelius Plantinga, *Not the Way It's Supposed to Be: A Breviary of Sin* (Grand Rapids: William B. Eerdmans Publishing Co., 1995).
7. Dallas Willard, *The Divine Conspiracy: Rediscovering Our Hidden Life in God* (San Francisco: HarperCollins, 1998), 37.
8. John Wesley, "The End of Christ's Coming," *Works* 2:483.
9. John Wesley, "A Letter to the Reverend Dr. Conyers Middleton," *Works* (J) 10:72.
10. John Wesley, "The New Birth," *Works* 2:187.
11. Other terms for Christian perfection include *full salvation* and *perfect love*.
12. John Wesley, "Brief Thoughts on Christian Perfection," *Works* (J) 11:446.
13. John Wesley, "A Plain Account of Christian Perfection," *Works* (J) 11:444.
14. Robin Maas, *Crucified Love: The Practice of Christian Perfection* (Nashville: Abingdon Press, 1989). 30.
15. John Wesley, "On Faith" (Heb. 11:6), *Works* 3:501.

Notes to Chapter 2

1. Martin Thornton, *The Rock and the River: An Encounter Between Traditional Spirituality and Modern Thought* (New York: Morehouse-Barlow Co., 1965), 30-31.
2. John Wesley, "The General Spread of the Gospel," *Works* 2:489.
3. Philip Yancey, *Reaching for the Invisible God* (Grand Rapids: Zondervan Publishing House, 2000), 182.
4. For a detailed analysis see Henry H. Knight III, *The Presence of God in the Christian Life: John Wesley and the Means of Grace* (Metuchen, N.J.: Scarecrow Press, 1992), 29-36.
5. John Wesley, "Letter to John Smith" (June 25, 1746), *Works* 26:201.
6. John Wesley, "On Dissipation," *Works* 3:120.
7. John Wesley, "Walking by Sight and Walking by Faith," *Works* 4:58.
8. Wesley, "On Dissipation," *Works* 3:118.
9. Yancey, *Reaching for the Invisible God*, 189.
10. John Wesley, "The Nature of Enthusiasm," *Works* 2:53.
11. Ibid., *Works* 2:54-55.
12. Ibid., *Works* 2:55-56.
13. Ibid., *Works* 2:59-60.
14. John Wesley, "The Means of Grace," *Works* 1:381.
15. For a detailed description see Knight, *The Presence of God in the Christian Life*, 2-5.

Notes to Chapter 3

1. Richard J. Foster, *Prayer: Finding the Heart's True Home* (San Francisco: HarperCollins, 1992), 1.
2. Ibid., 2.
3. John Wesley, "Letter to Miss March" (March 29, 1760), *The Letters of the Rev. John Wesley, A.M.*, ed. John Telford (London: The Epworth Press, 1931), 4:90.
4. John Wesley, *Notes*, I Thessalonians 5:16.
5. M. Robert Mulholland Jr., *Invitation to a Journey: A Road Map for Spiritual Formation* (Downers Grove, Ill.: InterVarsity Press, 1993), 105.
6. Ibid.
7. Ibid., 106.
8. Steve Harper, *Prayer and Devotional Life of United Methodists* (Nashville: Abingdon Press, 1999), 41.
9. John Wesley, "The Character of a Methodist," *Works* 9:37.
10. John Wesley, "The Great Privilege of those that are Born of God," *Works* 1:434.
11. John Wesley, "The Wilderness State," *Works* 2:209.

12. Wesley, *Notes,* 1 Thessalonians 5:16.
13. Richard J. Foster, *Celebration of Discipline: The Path to Spiritual Growth* (San Francisco: Harper & Row, 1978), 30.
14. John Wesley, "The Means of Grace," *Works* 1:384-85.
15. Wesley, *Notes,* Matthew 6:8.
16. Harper, *Prayer and Devotional Life of United Methodists,* 30.
17. Foster, *Celebration of Discipline,* 30.
18. Bill Hybels, *Too Busy Not to Pray: Slowing Down to Be with God* (Downers Grove, Ill.: InterVarsity Press, 1988), 7.
19. Ibid., 97-106. See also Marjorie J. Thompson, *Soul Feast* (Louisville, Ky.: Westminster John Knox Press, 1995), 35.
20. Harper, *Prayer and Devotional Life of United Methodists,* 28.
21. Foster, *Prayer,* 8.
22. Ibid., 9.
23. Ibid., 15.
24. Among the best of these resources is Roberta C. Bondi, *A Place to Pray: Reflections on the Lord's Prayer* (Nashville: Abingdon Press, 1998).
25. John Wesley, "Letter to Miss Bishop" (September 19, 1773), *Works* (J) 13:25.
26. Steve Harper, *Devotional Life in the Wesleyan Tradition* (Nashville: The Upper Room, 1983), 21.
27. Ibid., 22.

Notes to Chapter 4

1. Albert C. Outler, "Introduction," *Works* 1:57.
2. John Wesley, *Notes,* Colossians 3:16.
3. Marjorie J. Thompson, *Soul Feast: An Invitation to the Christian Spiritual Life* (Louisville, Ky.: Westminster John Knox Press, 1995), 18.
4. M. Robert Mulholland Jr., *Shaped by the Word: The Power of Scripture in Spiritual Formation* (Nashville: The Upper Room, 1985), 53.
5. Ibid., 91.
6. Ibid., 91-92.
7. I develop these themes about narrative in Scripture at greater length in *A Future for Truth: Evangelical Theology in a Postmodern World* (Nashville: Abingdon Press, 1997), chapter 6.
8. John Wesley, "Minutes of Several Conversations Between the Rev. Mr. Wesley and Others," *Works* (J) 8:323.
9. These include Steve Harper, *Prayer and Devotional Life of United Methodists* (Nashville: Abingdon Press, 1999), 46-56; and Thompson, *Soul Feast,* 22-25.
10. Henry H. Knight III, *The Presence of God in the Christian Life: John*

Wesley and the Means of Grace (Metuchen, N.J.: Scarecrow Press, 1992), 150-53; and Mulholland, *Shaped by the Word*, chapter 11.

11. John Wesley, "Preface, Notes on the Old Testament," *Works* (J) 14: 253.
12. Mulholland, *Shaped by the Word*, 21.
13. Wesley, "Preface, Notes on the Old Testament," *Works* (J) 14:253.
14. Ibid.
15. Thompson, *Soul Feast*, 23.
16. John Wesley, "Preface, Sermons on Several Occasions," *Works* 1:106.
17. Wesley, "Preface, Notes on the Old Testament," *Works* (J) 14: 253.
18. Ibid.

Notes to Chapter 5

1. Lining the Psalms means that a leader sings out a line of a Psalm and the congregation then sings it in response. This can be done well, but commonly was not in Wesley's day.
2. John Wesley, "Preface, Sermons on Several Occasions," *Works* 1:104.
3. John Wesley, "Reasons Against a Separation," *Works* 9:339.
4. Robert E. Webber, *Worship Is a Verb: Eight Principles for a Highly Participatory Worship* (Nashville: Star Song Publishing Group, 1992), 15.
5. Sally Morgenthaler, *Worship Evangelism* (Grand Rapids: Zondervan Publishing House, 1995), 47.
6. Gerrit Gustafson, "Worship Evangelism," *Psalmist* (Feb.–Mar. 1991), 31.
7. Robert Webber, *Signs of Wonder* (Nashville: Star Song Publishing Group, 1992), 33.
8. Henry H. Knight III, "Worship and Sanctification," *Wesleyan Theological Journal* 32:2 (fall 1997), 7.
9. Don E. Saliers, *Worship as Theology: Foretaste of Glory Divine* (Nashville: Abingdon Press, 1994), 96.
10. James F. White, *Introduction to Christian Worship,* rev. ed. (Nashville: Abingdon Press, 1990), 29.
11. Morgenthaler, *Worship Evangelism*, 48.
12. Webber, *Worship Is a Verb*, 17.
13. *The United Methodist Hymnal* (Nashville: The United Methodist Publishing House, 1989), 2.
14. M. Robert Mulholland Jr., *Invitation to a Journey: A Road Map for Spiritual Formation* (Downers Grove, Ill.: InterVarsity Press, 1993), 146.
15. Don E. Saliers, *Worship Come to Its Senses* (Nashville: Abingdon Press, 1996), 92.
16. *The United Methodist Hymnal*, 9-11.

Notes to Chapter 6

1. John Wesley, *Journal* (Aug. 11, 1755), *Works* 21:23.
2. *The United Methodist Book of Worship* (Nashville: The United Methodist Publishing House, 1992), 288-94.
3. Henry H. Knight III, *The Presence of God in the Christian Life: John Wesley and the Means of Grace* (Metuchen, N.J.: Scarecrow Press, 1992), 189-90. For a full discussion see David Tripp, *The Renewal of the Covenant in the Methodist Tradition* (London: The Epworth Press, 1969).
4. *The United Methodist Hymnal* (Nashville: The United Methodist Publishing House, 1989), 50-53.
5. Ibid., 50.
6. Ibid., 607.
7. Lester Ruth, *A Little Heaven Below: Worship at Early Methodist Quarterly Meetings* (Nashville: Kingswood Books, 2000), 110. See the full discussion on pp. 104-18.
8. John Wesley, "A Plain Account of the People Called Methodists," *Works* 9:267-68.
9. *The United Methodist Book of Worship*, 581-84.
10. Richard P. Heitzenrater, *The Elusive Mr. Wesley*, volume 1 (Nashville: Abingdon Press, 1984), 140.
11. Ibid., 142. For a full discussion of Wesley's views on healing see E. Brooks Holifield, *Health and Medicine in the Methodist Tradition* (New York: Crossroad, 1986), chapter 2.
12. John Wesley, *Journal* (May 18, 1772), *Works* 22:324.
13. *The United Methodist Book of Worship*, 613-29.
14. These include James K. Wagner, *Blessed to Be a Blessing* (Nashville: The Upper Room, 1980); James K. Wagner, *An Adventure in Healing and Wholeness* (Nashville: The Upper Room, 1993); and Tilda Norberg and Robert D. Webber, *Stretch Out Your Hand* (Nashville: The Upper Room, 1998).
15. Wagner, *Blessed to Be a Blessing* 29.
16. Good resources on healing from a charismatic perspective include Francis MacNutt, *Healing* (Altamonte Springs, Fla.: Cretion House, 1988) and Ken Blue, *Authority to Heal* (Downers Grove, Ill.: InterVarsity Press, 1987).

Notes to Chapter 7

1. Robert Wuthnow, *Sharing the Journey: Support Groups and America's New Quest for Community* (New York: The Free Press, 1994), 4.
2. Ibid., 6.

3. Ibid., 3.
4. Ibid., 4.
5. Ibid., 6 and 13.
6. Ibid., 14.
7. Ibid., 3.
8. Ibid., 7.
9. Ibid., 255.
10. Ibid., 4.
11. Ibid., 27.
12. "General Rules of the United Societies," *Works* 9:69-73.
13. David Lowes Watson, *The Early Methodist Class Meeting* (Nashville: Discipleship Resources, 1985), 97. For other important discussions of Wesley's small groups, see D. Michael Henderson, *John Wesley's Class Meeting: A Model for Making Disciples* (Nappanee, Ind.: Evangel Publishing House, 1997) and Howard A. Snyder, *Signs of the Spirit: How God Reshapes the Church* (Grand Rapids: Zondervan Publishing House, 1989).
14. John Wesley, "A Plain Account of the People Called Methodist," *Works* 9:266.
15. Ibid., 262.
16. Ibid.
17. See the account in George G. Hunter III, *Church for the Unchurched* (Nashville: Abingdon Press, 1996), 81-117. One of the earliest calls for small groups was Howard A. Snyder, *The Problem of Wineskins* (Downers Grove, Ill.: InterVarsity Press, 1975). Other notable resources are Dale E. Galloway, *20/20 Vision: How to Create a Successful Church* (Portland, Ore.: Scott Publishing, 1986), Jeffrey Arnold, *Starting Small Groups: Building Communities that Matter* (Nashville: Abingdon Press, 1977), and Craig Kennet Miller, *NextChurch.Now: Creating New Faith Communities* (Nashville: Discipleship Resources, 2000), chapter 8.
18. Key advocates of the "cell church" include Carl F. George, *Prepare Your Church for the Future* (Grand Rapids: Fleming H. Revell, 1991), Ralph W. Neighbour Jr., *Where Do We Go from Here?: A Guidebook for Cell Group Churches* (Houston, Tex.: Touch Publications, 1990), and Larry Stockstill, *The Cell Church* (Ventura, Calif.: Regal Books, 1998).
19. See the types of small groups discussed in Palmer Becker, *Called to Care* (Scottdale, Pa.: Herald Press, 1993) and Jeffrey Arnold, *Small Group Outreach* (Downers Grove, Ill.: InterVarsity Press, 1998).
20. Michael Slaughter, *Spiritual Entrepreneurs: Six Principles for Risking Renewal* (Nashville: Abingdon Press, 1994), 71-76.
21. Dick Wills, *Waking to God's Dream: Spiritual Leadership and Church Renewal* (Nashville: Abingdon Press, 1999), 43. See the entire discussion on 35-47.
22. David Lowes Watson, *Covenant Discipleship: Christian Formation*

Through Mutual Accountability (Nashville: Discipleship Resources, 1991), 78.

23. These include David Lowes Watson, *Forming Christian Disciples: The Role of Covenant Discipleship and Class Leaders in the Congregation* (Nashville: Discipleship Resources, 1989), and Gayle Watson, *Guide for Covenant Discipleship Groups* (Nashville: Discipleship Resources, 2000).

24. Henry H. Knight III and Don E. Saliers, *The Conversation Matters: Why United Methodists Should Talk with One Another* (Nashville: Abingdon Press, 1999).

25. Among the best are Lovett H. Weems Jr., *John Wesley's Message Today* (Nashville: Abingdon Press, 1992), Steve Harper, *John Wesley's Message for Today* (Grand Rapids: Zondervan, 1983), and Kenneth L. Carder, *Living Our Beliefs: The United Methodist Way* (Nashville: Discipleship Resources, 1996). An excellent companion to the study of the Articles of Religion (or as a study on its own) is Ted A. Campbell, *Methodist Doctrine: The Essentials* (Nashville: Abingdon Press, 1999).

26. See Knight and Saliers, *The Conversation Matters*, 63-74.

27. See John Wesley, "The Preface to Sermons on Several Occasions," *Works* 1:103-107.

Notes to Chapter 8

1. John Wesley, "The Danger of Riches," *Works* 3:230-31.

2. E. Stanley Jones, *The Unshakable Kingdom and the Unchanging Person* (Nashville: Abingdon Press, 1972), 116.

3. Richard J. Foster, *Celebration of Discipline: The Path to Spiritual Growth* (San Francisco: Harper & Row, 1978), 70.

4. Ronald J. Sider, *Rich Christians in an Age of Hunger: Moving from Affluence to Generosity* (Dallas: Word Publishing, 1997), 199.

5. Wesley, "The Use of Money," *Works* 2:278-79.

6. Harold Rogers, *Harry Denman: A Biography* (Nashville: The Upper Room, 1977), 76.

7. Wesley, "The Use of Money," *Works* 2:279.

8. Sider, *Rich Christians in an Age of Hunger,* 193-94.

9. Marjorie J. Thompson, *Soul Feast: An Invitation to the Christian Spiritual Life* (Louisville, Ky.: Westminster John Knox Press, 1995), 73.

10. Ibid., 71.

11. Wesley, "Upon Our Lord's Sermon on the Mount, VII," *Works* 1:593-594.

12. Ibid., *Works* 1:609.

13. Foster, *Celebration of Discipline,* 52.

14. Thompson, *Soul Feast*, 75.
15. Wesley, "Upon Our Lord's Sermon on the Mount, VII," *Works* 1:595.
16. Steve Harper, *Devotional Life in the Wesleyan Tradition* (Nashville: The Upper Room, 1983), 50.
17. Wesley, "Upon Our Lord's Sermon on the Mount, VII," *Works* 1:595.
18. Harper, *Devotional Life in the Wesleyan Tradition*, 51.
19. Wesley, "Upon Our Lord's Sermon on the Mount, VII," *Works* 1:595.
20. Dallas Willard, *The Spirit of the Disciplines: Understanding How God Changes Lives* (San Francisco: Harper & Row, 1988), 166.
21. Wesley, "Upon Our Lord's Sermon on the Mount, VII," *Works* 1:610.
22. Ibid., *Works* 1:598.
23. Willard, *The Spirit of the Disciplines*, 167.
24. Wesley, "Upon Our Lord's Sermon on the Mount, VII," *Works* 1:599-600.
25. Thompson, *Soul Feast*, 76-77.
26. Foster, *Celebration of Discipline*, 48.

Notes to Chapter 9

1. Ronald J. Sider, *Good News and Good Works: A Theology for the Whole Gospel* (Grand Rapids: Baker Books, 1993), 26.
2. Douglas Strong, *They Walked in the Spirit: Personal Faith and Social Action in America* (Louisville, Ky.: Westminster John Knox Press, 1997).
3. E. Stanley Jones, *The Unshakable Kingdom and the Unchanging Person* (Nashville: Abingdon Press, 1972), 40.
4. Donald W. Dayton, *Discovering an Evangelical Heritage* (New York: Harper & Row, 1976).
5. John Wesley, "The Rules of the United Societies," *Works* 9:72.
6. "Social Principles," paragraphs 64-70 (pp. 84-106), *The Book of Discipline of The United Methodist Church 1996* (Nashville: The United Methodist Publishing House, 1996).
7. Jones, *Unshakable Kingdom*, 54.
8. Michael Slaughter, *Spiritual Entrepreneurs: Six Principles for Risking Renewal* (Nashville: Abingdon Press, 1994), 55.
9. Ibid., 56.
10. John Wesley, "On Visiting the Sick," *Works* 3:387-88.
11. Dick Wills, *Waking to God's Dream: Spiritual Leadership and Church Renewal* (Nashville: Abingdon Press, 1999), 31.
12. Ibid., 32.
13. John Wesley, "The General Deliverance," *Works* 2:440.
14. Ibid., *Works* 2:442.
15. Tony Campolo, *How to Rescue the Earth Without Worshiping Nature* (Nashville: Thomas Nelson Publishers, 1992), 138.

16. Ibid., 141.
17. Ronald J. Sider, *Living Like Jesus: Eleven Essentials for Growing a Genuine Faith* (Grand Rapids: Baker Books, 1996), 125.
18. Tony Campolo, *Is Jesus a Republican or a Democrat?* (Dallas: Word Publishing, 1995), 1-16.

Notes to Chapter 10

1. Mortimer Arias, *Announcing the Reign of God* (Philadelphia: Fortress Press, 1984), 2.
2. H. Eddie Fox and George E. Morris, *Let the Redeemed of the Lord Say So!* (rev. ed.) (Franklin, Tenn.: Providence House Publishers, 1999), xvi.
3. Ibid.
4. Rebeca Manley Pippert, *Out of the Saltshaker & into the World* (Downers Grove, Ill.: InterVarsity Press, 1999), 9.
5. H. Eddie Fox and George E. Morris, *Faith-Sharing: Dynamic Christian Witnessing by Invitation* (rev. & exp. ed.) (Nashville: Discipleship Resources, 1996), 92.
6. Ibid., 89-90.
7. Ibid., 95. For an extended discussion of the role of listening see Ronald W. Johnson, *How Will They Hear If We Don't Listen?* (Nashville: Broadman & Holman Publishers, 1994).
8. Pippert, *Out of the Saltshaker & into the World*, 80.
9. Fox and Morris, *Faith-Sharing*, 103 (paraphrasing Denman).
10. Ibid., 104.
11. Ibid., 105-13.
12. Ibid., 115-28. See also Pippert, *Out of the Saltshaker & into the World*, 186-96.
13. The best resource in my opinion is Fox and Morris, *Faith-Sharing*. Besides the book there is a Faith-Sharing Video Kit, also available from Discipleship Resources. Other excellent resources include Rodney E. Wilmoth, *How United Methodists Share Their Faith* (Nashville: Abingdon Press, 1999) and Richard Stoll Armstrong, *Service Evangelism* (Philadelphia: The Westminster Press, 1979).
14. Roger K. Swanson and Shirley F. Clement, *The Faith-Sharing Congregation: Developing a Strategy for the Congregation as Evangelist* (Nashville: Discipleship Resources, 1996), is one good example.
15. For an extended discussion of the theology and practice of hospitality see Christine D. Pohl, *Making Room: Recovering Hospitality as a Christian Tradition* (Grand Rapids: William B. Eerdmans Publishing Co., 1999).

Notes

16. Swanson and Clement, *The Faith-Sharing Congregation*, 25.
17. Ibid., 18.
18. Pippert, *Out of the Saltshaker & into the World*, 93.
19. Swanson and Clement, *The Faith-Sharing Congregation*, 8.
20. Ibid., 24.
21. George G. Hunter III, "The 'Celtic' Way for Evangelizing Today," *Journal of the Academy for Evangelism in Theological Education* 13 (1997–1998), 15. See also Hunter's discussion in his *How to Reach Secular People* (Nashville: Abingdon Press, 1992), 81-91.
22. William J. Abraham, *The Logic of Evangelism* (Grand Rapids: William B. Eerdmans Publishing Co., 1989), 13.
23. Ibid., chapters 5-7.
24. Daniel T. Benedict, *Come to the Waters: Baptism and Our Ministry of Welcoming Seekers & Making Disciples* (Nashville: Discipleship Resources, 1996).
25. Michael Slaughter, *Spiritual Entrepreneurs* (Nashville: Abingdon Press, 1994), 72.